Praise for *Spirit, Mind and*

"In her new book Spirit, Mind & Money Dawn DelVecchio delivers some of the best wisdom for coaches and holistic practitioners anywhere. The new perspectives will enable the members of the heart-centered community to build their businesses in a powerful way, and finally be paid what they are worth. This book is a breath of fresh air, in great contrast to traditional marketing books that don't often speak to the transformational market. It's essential reading for the new (or stuck) practitioner!"

— **Pamela Bruner**, Best Selling Author, 7-Figure Success Coach and Founder of Make Your Success Real Coaching www.makeyoursuccessreal.com

"This book is sure to ignite some fires ... Dawn DelVecchio slays a "sacred cow" (finally someone did it!) that holds way too many spiritually-minded entrepreneurs back: that money is bad and wanting money is beneath the morals of the enlightened. With her "Ineffective Business Mindsets" and "Unexamined Money Mantras" the author reveals the mental-emotional disconnect that disempowers gifted experts by keeping them caught in a cycle of economic struggle. An essential read for any helper, healer or service-provider who wants to make money by doing good in the world."

— **Loral Langemeier**, International Wealth Expert and 5-time, NY Times Best-Selling Author.

"At last a book that tackles the numerous misconceptions around money and spirituality. A must read for every heart-centered entrepreneur!"

— **Dr. Joy Martina**, Wholistic Psychologist and author of Sleep Your Fat Away.

"Spirit, Mind & Money isn't just a book for "holistic business owners" ... it's a Holistic approach to business! I've finally found a book on "business" that doesn't bore me to tears or clash with my values. The downright honesty about what it takes to grow a small business is greatly appreciated within the pages of Spirit, Mind & Money. Having worked directly with Dawn during my last business growth period, I realised the value of experience that Dawn brings to the courage required in becoming a 'business-minded person."

— **Caroline Muir**, Author of Tantra, The Art of Conscious Loving and Tantra Goddess, A Memoir of Sexual Awakening Founder of Divine Feminine Awakening www.divine-feminine.com

"In turmoil about translating your purpose into a viable business? Frustrated with the monthly challenge of making ends meet? Struggling to get ahead or keep up? Dawn DelVecchio's insights show you specific action steps to take to permanently leave behind the conundrum of high-service and low income. Spirit, Mind & Money brings you practical tools and the mindset adjustments you need to take a sacred vision or purpose and convert it into a financially stable and rewarding business. Dawn has done it. She'll show you how too."

— **Dr. Ken Christian**, Best Selling Author and Founder of Max Potential Project www.drkenchristian.com

"Dawn DelVecchio has hit the mark with Spirit, Mind & Money, providing a solid path for holistic business owners to follow. The book helps them not only share their message and mission in a powerful way, it shows them how to receive the financial rewards that they are meant to enjoy. Throughout the book, readers are given the opportunity to remain connected to their spiritual path, become aware of thoughts and patterns relevant to their relationship with money and then, gently guided to move forward on the business side with step by step instructions. If you've got a big dream for your business (and life!) but your numbers aren't adding up to prosperity, Spirit, Mind & Money is a must read for you!"

— **Nancy Matthews**, Founder of Women's Prosperity Network.

"While in medical school, there was very little education or guidance given on how to operate a profitable practice. Money is a subject that doesn't get tackled head-on nearly often enough, yet it's also one of the biggest challenges people are facing. This book lets you face money in a more aware, clear and holistic way."

— **Jessica Hayman**, N.D. Licensed Naturopathic Doctor, Sedona, Arizona

"Reading Spirit, Mind & Money has inspired me to tighten the focus of my marketing more specifically on my clients' greatest challenges. For starters, my website homepage will soon feature a welcome video, an opt-in gift and a whole lot less clutter! I found Dawn's insights on how to reframe limited thinking about money especially valuable. Her writing style is warm, clear and encouraging, and the included worksheets make her helpful information easy to personalize and apply. Your investment in Spirit, Mind & Money could easily pay for itself in increased income a thousand times over — for starters!"

— **Benjamin Bernstein**, Owner, astrologer, shamanic healer & awakening activator www.AstroShaman.com

"Spirit, Mind & Money leaves the spiritually-inclined reader motivated and confident in taking steps toward whatever it is we want. I found the Money Mindset Reframes in chapter eleven particularly choice content; once we realize that we are the source of our success, the small, everyday practices are required to keep us persistent."

— **Leslie Flowers**, speaker and author of Champion, 21st Century Women, Guardians of Wealth & Legacy

"Being a 'busy' business owner and single mother, I began the book with the notion of breezing through a bit of it, anticipating setting it aside to move on with something "more meaningful" or perhaps "more relevant", or even "something that will net me instant epiphanies and reward". As I began to read I couldn't put the book down. I saw myself in it, I saw other businesses and clients in it, and I forged on, finishing the book in record time. Digesting. Assimilating. And now beginning to go back through to highlight, strategize, make changes, capitalize on strengths and change my weaknesses. I canceled my planned advertising, based on the book and the light bulb as to who my client is, what motivates them, how I communicate, and what they need. Wow. Thank you, Dawn DelVecchio, for sharing your insight, experience, and simplicity with us to enhance not only the business owners experience, but also the consumer/clients."

— **Dr. Mimi Chatwood**, Owner and Founder of Bliss Chiropractic

"Dawn is a great teacher. And what I love about her is her willingness to always teach and share what she has learned either through her own experiences, or from the greats. If you're looking to grow (or start) a business and want to hack the process, Spirit, Mind & Money is a great start and one that will bear valuable lessons."

— **Veena Sidhu**, Co-founder of Authentic Woman
www.authentic-woman.com

"Entrepreneurship books are often crammed with too much heart or too much brains, at the expense of the other. Spirit, Mind & Money hits that rare sweet spot between the two, empowering small business owners with a holistic game plan for igniting the kind of personal and planetary impact that leaves them both better entrepreneurs and better human beings."

— **Omar Michael**, copywriting & marketing consultant & former head copywriter of Mindvalley.

"Wow! Spirit, Mind & Money is a Holistic approach to business that is authentic and honest. This easy to read book gives great insights on how to create and become a thriving holistic business owner. Dawn truly has a heart-centered approach and writing style, yet a realistic business mindset. She will not only help you to turn your gifts into a profitable business, she will give you the tools you need to confidently step up and charge what your unique gifts and talents are worth."

— **Patricia Miller**, Transformative Coach and Founder of Whole Wisdom Whole YOU coaching.

"Spirit, Mind & Money changed my life! Reading it was the final push I needed to stop letting my fears and excuses hold me back from running the business (and living the life) I've always wanted. This book has really opened my eyes to the ways I've been undermining my own success as a holistic healer. Now I can make small changes in my mindset and actions to have a much bigger impact - and more enjoyment doing what I do best!"

— **Amanda Amethyst**, Healer & Coach, Amethyst Alchemy Healing

"As a beginner in the business world, this book really showed me how to take charge of my own success and say goodbye to the slavery of employment. And it was fun to read as well!"

— **Cher Duclos**, Owner/Designer of Sweet Life Threads, Handmade Upcycled Clothing

"This book is a wonderful new opportunity for women to see their worth and understand their relationship to money. For too many years we have been marginalized and paid less than our male counterparts. I believe this is part of why we have this disconnect about money and making the amount we deserve! Dawn DelVecchio has opened a door to a new and innovative way of thinking about money and wealth. Her writing style is easy to read and incorporate into your daily life! I highly recommend this book to anyone who is looking to grow and fulfill their financial potential."

— **Bryna Pauker**, LCSW, OSW-C, ACHP-SW Author of Fifty Days to Fifty: A Personal Journey

"If only Dawn DelVecchio had written Spirit, Mind & Money years ago when I was just getting started as a coach! At the time, my desire to make a world-changing impact was perpetually hobbled by the quagmire of unconscious beliefs I had around money, marketing, and business ... With clarity, compassion, and an uncommon willingness to debunk commonly held myths and misconceptions, Dawn hands passionate yet broke, holistic business owners what they need to finally turn their calling into a financially flourishing business."

— **Susanna Maida**, Ph.D., Founder and Visionary Business Weaver at www.ReWeavingTheWorld.com

Spirit, Mind and Money:

A New Conversation About Service and Success for the Holistic Business Owner

Dawn DelVecchio

Names, locations and types of businesses associated with illustrative stories in this book have been changed to protect the privacy of individuals and businesses. In many cases, a compilation of 2 or more stories or skill sets has been combined to further respect individual privacy. If you think you recognize someone in the pages of this book, I assure you, you do not.

SPIRIT, MIND AND MONEY: A NEW CONVERSATION ABOUT SERVICE AND SUCCESS FOR THE HOLISTIC BUSINESS OWNER

Library of Congress Control Number: 2015913702

ISBN (978-0-9861174-9-7)

Printed in USA by Dawn DelVecchio

For People Ready to Eliminate Financial Blocks to Business Success ...

RE:Visioning Your Inner Blueprint

A Special Gift from Dawn

RE:Visioning

"A Simple Way to RE*view* and RE*vise* your Inner "Vision" of Money, Service & Success, so you can Eliminate Financial Struggle, Make a Bigger Difference with your Gifts, and Grow a Business that Lets you *THRIVE!*"

RE:Visioning is a powerful method for eliminating harmful programming of any kind – at a subconscious level. The process is easy to do and ideal for the heart-centered visionary who longs to bring their gifts to the world in a bigger way, but struggles with financial limitation.

http://www.SpiritMindMoneyBook.com/re-vision

You can use the **RE:Visioning** process to ...

- ✓ Eliminate negative, subconscious programming about money .
- ✓ Effectively *do* what you came here to do, and thrive in the process.
- ✓ Swiftly transform your inner conversation around money so that it serves the highest GOOD of all.
- ✓ Set up a new *operating system* around abundance.
- ✓ Take effective, integrated action to earn the money you need.
- ✓ Transform your relationship to Money, Service and Success!

Grab Your Own Inner Blueprint for Success with a Complimentary Copy of the **RE:Visioning** Process

Access your copy and start your RE:Visioning right away, simply go to:

http://www.SpiritMindMoneyBook.com/re-vision

Dedication

This book is dedicated to the many clients, students, holistic visionaries and small business owners who have crossed my path. You have taught me much.

It's also dedicated to the countless numbers of people awakening to a new way of living on Planet Earth – a way that's more WHOLE, and SUSTAINABLE. You are the ones who are here to lead us, and this book is intended to be a small part of the support you'll need to do it. This book is for you if you have or wish to have a small business that serves your community or our world. What you do, who you serve and what you provide doesn't matter as much as how you perceive business and money in the context of your work in the world.

From my Heart to yours – many blessings!

Dawn DelVecchio
Chiang Mai, Thailand, January 2015

Acknowledgments

As with any book, this couldn't have been written without the love, support, guidance and occasional smack upside the head by family, mentors and friends.

Specifically, I want to thank and acknowledge my mom and dad, without whom, who knows what would have become of me. For they adopted me as an infant, raised me fully and completely as their own, then loved me without condition despite the fact that I was a radically different kind of person than anything for which they may have planned.

To my son, Zac, who gave me meaning and motivation to make something of value with my life. Despite my many mistakes as a young mom, you've become one hell of a great man and I'm proud to call you son.

To my beloved mate and soon-to-be-official husband Doug, your unconditional love, belief in me, steadfastness and mirth are a blessing for which I'm thankful for every day. You are my a-muse ... and my rock!

To the key players and mentors in my professional life whose guidance, role-modeling and opportunities have helped me actually BE, DO and HAVE a rich, fulfilling life, thank you.

In particular ...

Vishen Lakhiani, Founder of Mindvalley, for giving me the opportunity to learn internet marketing and hone my writing skills with some of the savviest young marketers in the industry.

Carol Kline, #1 New York Times bestselling author, coauthor of *Happy for No Reason* and five, *Chicken Soup for the Soul* books, for initiating me into then guiding me on the book writing journey.

Ajarn Chai, founder of the Thai Boxing Association of the USA, for reminding me always to believe in myself and for consistently encouraging women to be in our power amidst the male-dominated world of muaythai. My "grit" was honed well under your tutelage, sir!

I'd also like to thank the family and friends who read the manuscript for this book to offer feedback and guidance. Each of you added valuable insights and I thank you once again for taking the time and care. In particular, I want to call out Susanna Maida, Dr. Ken Christian and Kaileen Sherk. Your critical eyes helped me up-level the material immensely!

To my Team, Diana, Lisa, Doug, and Leslie, thank you for helping me in all aspects of getting this book from an idea to a reality. And to the many friends near and far: thank you for gifting my life!.

Preface

I've written this book based on the premise that your skills, services and vision are needed. At this juncture in our world, we need the Holistic Business Owners: the practitioners, healers, service-providers, coaches, visionaries and change-agents; to step up, play a bigger role in their communities and the world, and lead.

If Spirit/God/Divine had the wherewithal to seed a vision and purpose within you, then the same force of All That Is *absolutely* has the wherewithal to provide a thriving living for you.

But there's a caveat to that universal promise: *You* will have to cooperate with the vision. You will have to develop the business skills you need and clear up any contrary (often subconscious) beliefs, habits and excuses that can block your success.

And of course, you will have to take the actions needed to create a thriving business. Because without the ability to thrive, you will find yourself (as so many others have) giving with an empty vessel, helping very few and quite possibly, harming yourself.

When you use what is offered in this book to gain insight, you are taking the first step toward healing and wholing your relationship to **Money, Service, and Success.**

Some of what I share may challenge you. Some concepts you may disagree with. I only ask that you remain open-minded and remember: YOU are needed. I wrote this to help you *reach and serve* those who are waiting for you!

Table of Contents

INTRODUCTION
THE GREAT AWAKENING

"Where there's Fear there's Power. Passion is our Healer. Desire cracks open the Gate, if you're Ready it will take you Through."

This quote is part of an ancient chant to the Goddess. It came to me many years ago through the author, activist and ecofeminist, Starhawk. I was a young, single mom then. I sang this, and many other chants, in a circle of women, twice monthly.

There were six of us. We had all birthed sons at home in 1984. We were all awakening from a slumber of Americana and into a world of the Sacred Earth, Sacred Feminine and the desire for something more than our culture promised.

These were the early days of the re-awakening — the days when recycling was a rebel novelty, using diet to heal was suspect, and conversations around feminine power were unwelcome in most circles.

Back then, my scholarly feminist professors dismissed "goddess talk" as embarrassingly woo-woo in *serious* conversations.

Yet today, we can look back to the 1980s and see that, in pockets across many parts of the world, folks were *awakening* to something else. Whether it was through ecology, health and nutrition, Eastern medicine, philosophy and religions, activism in response to the crisis of cold war nuclear armament, or in my case, sacred feminine spirituality ... the seeds planted in the 1960s had begun to sprout.

Today I marvel at the way we can talk about alternative and complementary medicine in most circles without a blink. I sigh with relief and gratitude for the early organic farmers and shoppers who literally rooted safe food amidst the insanity of genetic modification. I'm delighted that things like recycling, nutrition, yoga and meditation have gone mainstream. Even my 83 year old dad now knows what *Shiv asana* is, thanks to senior's yoga!

Those were the formative years of what is today, a full-fledged, here-to-stay, way of life for millions of people world-wide. Living sustainably on Mother Earth, buying organic, going to chiropractors, Traditional Chines Medicine (TCM), or other non-allopathic doctors and incorporating healthy lifestyle habits have all become a part of the conversation.

Spirituality has gained tremendous depth and breadth as well. No longer do the trite answers and shallow threats of mainstream religion work to keep the Awakening Ones in line. We seek deeper meaning and connection within ourselves, with our health and vitality, our family and friends and with the Divine, however we may experience it.

Whether you call it Conscious Living, a Holistic Lifestyle or something else doesn't matter. What does matter is that an ever-increasing percentage of the population — in the western world, at least — is turning toward a more sustainable, meaningful way of BE-ing.

We simply cannot buy into the promise of eternal consumer happiness anymore. We see through the veil of a fear-based world. The little man behind the curtain has been revealed, and the great and powerful Oz, of a false bliss, no longer compels us.

As more and more people in the Western *and* Eastern world turn away from an unsustainable, unfulfilling mindset ... they must be served.

Which leads to you: the small business owner.

You. A Holistic Business Owner?

A Holistic Business Owner can be an author, speaker, teacher, product- or service-provider, store owner, performer, ceremonialist or healer. They can be coaches, financial planners, attorneys, or copywriters and marketing consultants like me. What we share are the high intentions to do good in the world. And we are often drawn to our work because it has great meaning for us on a soul level.

We are the ones who connect our work with our life mission or Soul Purpose. We make a connection between our outer work in the world (our business) and our greater purpose.

I wrote this book for you, no matter your business. You need not be a holistic health practitioner, organic farmer or meditation teacher to find and gain support for your business within these pages.

This book is for you if you have or wish to have a small business that serves your community or our world. What you do, who you serve and what you provide doesn't matter as much as how you *perceive business and money* in the context of your work in the world.

The awakening masses are looking for a lot more than alternative medicine and organic foods. From car mechanics to pet store owners, style consultants to landscapers, they're looking for products, programs and service providers who "get it" — people who understand their values and needs, respect them and speak the language of whole/holistic consciousness.

In the context of this book I am using the term "Holistic Business Owner" to refer to business owners who share a common set of values. More than just holistic *practitioners*, this includes anyone who is of service to their community or world, and who values a more well-rounded approach to living than what we are offered via mainstream services, media and medicine.

That's quite a wide span of folks, I know. But the common thread here are the values. These values may include things like:

- A holistic approach to health and well-being.
- An appreciation for nature and respect for the environment.
- A recognition that true health and happiness come from a balanced lifestyle.
- An understanding that we are more than just a body and mind, and therefore must give time to our spiritual life.
- A sense of care for the planet, knowing it must be respected and protected in order to ensure quality of life for future generations.
- A recognition of the interconnectivity of all life.

ဆာ

Holistic Business Owners see the whole picture. We recognize and value the interconnectedness of all life and therefore live our lives in a manner that honors it all: Spirit, Mind and Body…we are also the ones who struggle the most when it comes to making our Soul Purpose work, a genuine business.

ဆာ

We are the ones who have questioned mainstream thinking about a host of issues — from petty politicking, engineered food, drug-focused medicine and institutionalized education.

The rationalist, materialist (AKA: Scientific) argument that we live in a disconnected universe made up of discrete, isolated parts, that matter is dead, and that there is no greater meaning to all of this doesn't make sense to us because we understand that the WHOLE is greater than the sum of its parts. We understand the UNITY beneath the seeming separateness.

In fact, if I had to name one single thing that is a common theme among Holistic Business Owners it is that we see (or seek to see) the whole picture. We recognize and value the interconnectedness of all life and therefore live our lives in a manner that honors it all: Spirit, Mind and Body.

Unfortunately, we are also the ones who struggle the most when it comes to making our Soul Purpose work a genuine business.

After many years and several failed businesses, I've come to the conclusion that a big part of why it is often the Holistic Business Owners who struggle most, is because we are the ones who have the most difficulty embracing the mindset of a business owner.

Without the right mindset, everything else crumbles. For to build and run a business requires the commitment to first value and then develop two very specific things:

1. The skill sets of a business owner, and
2. A healthy relationship with the lifeblood of business ... money.

And this is true *even* when we have been called to our business on a deeply personal, spiritual level.

And ... there's a glitch. A gap. A healing still to be done within this community. For as many of us rejected the old system of mindless consumerism, toxic solutions, cold war craziness and empty religious promises, we also threw out the very tool that could propel us from margin to center.

That tool is money.

The Spirit, Mind, and Money of Your Business

Simply put, for you to have business success, you will need the same things *all* successful business builders require: Tenacity and

Vision (the *Spirit* of your business); Strategic Planning, Marketing and Promotion (the *Mind* of your business); and Financial Maturity (the *Money* of your business.)

These requirements are necessary no matter how divinely guided is your mission and your message. Unfortunately, because we do in fact have high intentions, because we *do* feel called to our work and because we are focused on the positive ways we can help, many of us fall into a belief trap that undermines our ability to reach and serve others. If we don't address this *trap* head-on, it will prevent us from enjoying material success.

What is this trap? It's the belief that the spark of vision which inspired your business in the first place is enough, all by itself, to magically transport you right into success — without any business know-how, without any plan or strategy and without any honest soul-searching about false money beliefs.

What this looks like for many of us is something like this: We get the vision and inspiration, we invest (sometimes years of our lives and 10s of $1000s of dollars) in the skills of our trade and then we "check out" mentally when it's time to learn how to run a *business*.

In other words, while we are practical with acquiring the credentials to be of service, we become highly *impractical* when it comes to developing the skills, the mindset and the spirit needed for success.

Too many of us begin to believe in magic ... or what you might call "the Law of Attraction without Action." In other words, instead of learning business skills, we believe things like: the right people and circumstance will serendipitously cross our path and our business growth will be fluid. Or: we won't have to do any *outreach* or *marketing* to get customers or clients — they'll simply be *attracted* to us, thanks to our stellar intent and skills.

This kind of assumption spells disaster — financially, emotionally and energetically. It's a trap. When we don't attend to the Mind or

Money elements of our business, assuming they'll just spontaneously flow, the very opposite occurs most of the time.

And while magical people and circumstances WILL line up for you when YOU are lined up with the Spirit of your business, I have some harsh news: Flow and business success only happen when you approach your business holistically and give attention to the all important Mind and Money components as well.

The Law of Attraction *does* work. All the time, in fact. That's why if you want to attract consistent, *paying* clients and customers, you'll need to treat your business like a *business*.

In short, starting a business (no matter how much you love what you do) involves business-related work as well as inner work. You will get knocked down sometimes. You will have to make tough decisions — scary decisions — about money, work load, overhead, support and much more. This is why if you *really* want to run a successful business of any kind, you must be ready to grow and to ...

Slay Some Sacred Cows

"Mom, you've been busting your ass as long as I can remember." This is what my son said to me when I asked him if he thought I worked hard enough.

Why was I asking my 24 year old this kind of question? I was angry. I was frustrated. I was confused and pissed off and sick to death of being broke and struggling.

After all, I had worked very hard over the last 24 years to stabilize myself from poor, single mother to financial adult. Yet at 43, I was worse off than ever! Living with my parents after a horrific Spanish "fling" that sucked up my little remaining divorce settlement, I was barely able to rub two quarters together once my credit card bills were paid. I had thrown in the proverbial towel on men for good (or so I thought) and was disgusted with myself for the poor choices I had made.

I was angry that I still had nothing to show for how hard I had worked for more than 20 years, trying to make something of myself. I was furious that I still could not figure out how to create financial stability — a stability that seemed to come so easily to others.

Hard Work Wasn't Enough

I was raised in a hard-working family. My father worked in a factory and my mom as a legal secretary. My parents believed, like most employees, that to make money you had to work hard. To make a lot of money? You'd have to work really hard. All the adults around me instilled this belief in me and so, I went about trying to build one small business after another, *not* by developing business management skills, but simply by working friggin' hard.

I got nowhere.

Admittedly the divorce I went through in 2003 took a toll on me, as it does for so many ... especially women. In fact, we know that women's incomes and standard of living tend to plummet significantly following divorce, as compared to men.[1] In my case, since I had chosen to cut bait and run, rather than stick around to fight and suffer, that "plummet" was significantly deeper.

Still, that was more than five years ago! Since then, I had been slowly building a new career as a travel writer and magazine editor in the exotic orient. I should have had something to show for myself by now. I had worked so hard, written so much, given up so much.

But here I was, 43 ... and broke again.

---

[1] See http://www.bedrockdivorce.com/faq.php#impact and
https://www.oppenheimerfunds.com/articles/article_10-29-09-111649.jsp

Was I just lazy? Was I just not willing to do what it takes? Maybe this was the problem. And so I posed the question to my son in a moment of shear frustration.

Of course, he saw things differently. Zac's earliest years were colored by my college studies. It was there where I discovered that I had a knack for writing and communication.

As a young, single mother, I also had a knack for anxiety. I worried continually about school, life, my future, my son's future and money. To counter-act the fear, I took my studies very seriously. I figured I had better (yep, you guessed it) *work really hard* in school so I could get a good job when I graduated.

This was my son's first exposure, I would learn many years later, to "mom busting her butt." And it didn't stop there ...

When I graduated, my worries, confused beliefs about my own abilities, and impoverished attitude set me up for failure at the start. I could not find a job. Supposedly the economy was bad. I believed this at the time, but worked hard nonetheless, applying for numerous positions. For most, I was either under-qualified, ill-qualified or occasionally, *over* qualified.

I was smart, but I wasn't savvy. *Big difference.* When my family started encouraging me to take a postal worker job, I knew it was time to get outta Dodge. With no offense to postal workers, I really could not see myself, a woman with a BA degree who graduated with Honors, and a specialization in Feminist Literary Criticism, committing to a life as a public employee. All those hours of an unengaged mind sounded like a form of prolonged torture.

The Work Harder Myth

My decision: move away from the East Coast and try something new. So I moved my son and myself to Santa Fe, New Mexico. Not knowing what I would do or how I would get by, I took a job as a waitress in a breakfast joint before landing my first, career-like job as a Desk Top Publisher at Kinko's.

Fast forward a couple of years and life in Santa Fe for both Zac and I had changed dramatically. By then, we were both *working hard* as martial arts students. Zac was now old enough to join me, as we literally and physically busted our butts to become muaythai boxers (think kickboxing with elbows and knees).

I spent much of my time running the gym with my (now former) spouse. From the time my son was seven (and I was 26), the three of us spent the majority of our evenings and weekends training, exercising, sparring and running the business.

I had my own first real business then too. Taking what I learned at Kinko's, I went off on my own, providing desk top publishing services to small businesses in town. I did everything from designing brochures and menus, to teaching people how to use their computers for word processing; or typing manuscripts for authors. I charged very little for my work, having no understanding of the relative value of what I was offering. I was indeed busting butt: both to develop martial skills and bring in some cash.

The trouble was, without having any know-how for running a business, I charged too little, invested too little in business growth, and had no clue how to do things like manage finances, leverage my time, or market myself to build a client base. I simply created a job for myself that demanded long hours and paid a low wage — by the hour.

The Heart of a Fighter

Have you ever considered the possibility that obstacles are actually the Universe's way of strengthening you? Like a mighty sword of the finest steel, success is earned through a process of forging. And while I don't believe all growth is caused by adversity, let's face it, a cushy life doesn't necessarily lead to strength.

Just as strength in your body comes from challenging activities, strength of spirit and vision often come when we are tested. Fold under the first obstacle, and you won't get far.

ഇ)രു

If you are bootstrapping a business on vision and a small purse, you had better have the heart of a fighter if you want your business to survive.

ഇ)രു

This is why, to grow a thriving business — one that supports you and serves abundantly — you need to have the heart of a fighter. Let me explain ...

In time, my martial practice, rigorous fitness routine, daily running and lots of sparring, led to ring fighting. To this day I still argue that fighters have got to be some of the best trained athletes in the world. The power, stamina and plain old *grit* it takes to fight competitively is extreme. Either prepare, or expect to get hurt ... *badly*.

Ring fighting requires tremendous aerobic capacity, for starters. It also takes anaerobic explosiveness so that you can strike quick and hard. And of course, it takes a sharp and highly focused mind. You must field incoming attacks in a split second — second after second after second.

You also need super-quick recovery time, the mental-emotional fortitude to take a shot and not just avoid crumbling, but come back fighting. In other words, in order to even consider stepping into an amateur or professional ring fight, it takes busting your butt daily.

So for a woman who was raised to be a girl, the mental-emotional fortitude took just as much to cultivate as the athletic prowess did.

And here's where you, the small business owner comes in. They say a great fighter has "Heart" and it's true. Because when you step in that ring with one other woman or man facing you, you cannot, you *cannot* lose your shit. No matter what they throw at you.

Chin tucked, hands up, laser focus and the willingness to take a shot — or many — and come back swinging. This is what fighting is. And friends, let me tell you something: If you are bootstrapping a business on vision and a small purse, you had better have the heart of a fighter if you want your business to survive!

You WILL Get Knocked Down—Will You Get Back Up?

"I get knocked down, but I get up again, nothing's ever going to keep me down ... "

Chumbawumba – Tub Thumping

Starting a business will knock you down. It is no easy task to build a business on vision and personal will. (It's particularly difficult if you try to do it without any business skills!) You will have to learn how to scale up with limited budget and time. You will have to manage your life, your family, your health, when it feels like no one has your back. You will have to pay the bills, invest in things you don't yet have the money for and make scary decisions ... sometimes daily.

Running a business is *not* for dilettantes. Nor is it for people who believe their vision alone is enough. You've got to have the Heart and Spirit of a fighter. And this can make many folks who want to have a business very uncomfortable indeed. This is why it's not enough for your business to be a whim or dream or something in which you want to dabble.

You are Needed More than Ever

Today I live in Sedona, Arizona for most of the year. This is a town where mystics and energy healers have their own association, where psychics run billboard ads on the back of the tourist trolley and a store titled "Center for the New Age" is but one of many retail outlets where you can buy crystals, healing tools, books, jewelry and psychic readings. Our town is also blessed with a multitude of healers: Chiropractors, TCM Doctors, Massage Therapists and Energy Practitioners of all arrays, all calling Sedona home.

In other words, I live in Holistic Business Central. But long before I lived here, I valued the holistic and spiritual dimensions of life. As an Herbalist, Astrologer, Tarot Reader of 30 years and Goddess Ritual Facilitator, I knew a thing or two about holistic health and spirituality long before my Sedona days, or even my days in Santa Fe, where I raised my son and grew my martial arts skills all those years ago.

I live in Sedona for a reason: I value living in a place where spiritual and holistic practitioners are taken seriously. Unfortunately, many of these gifted healers and helpers are struggling financially. After all, it's expensive to live in such a stunningly beautiful, destination city.

But I will argue in this book that those external influences are not what we need to address. It's the inner conversation around money that's keeping so many people stuck. And I feel that addressing this inner conversation is urgent, because a new, more holistic approach to everything (pretty much) is needed. In fact, it is my heart-felt belief that ... *The Healers, Holistic Health Practitioners, Teachers, and*

Change Agents must come to the forefront of leadership at this critical time in human history.

Let's face it, our world has turned upside down and backward. For one thing, it's increasingly toxic, with frightfully dangerous poisons infecting land, air, water and food. Rampant, preventable lifestyle diseases like obesity, high blood pressure, hypertension, diabetes and even some cancers are diminishing the quality of people's lives, long before their time.

It's clear to many of us that the fragmented, mechanistic orientation of the western, scientific paradigm — and the allopathic medicine which is based on it — simply will not or cannot see the forest for the trees. Chemical drug companies still go about inventing side-effect-laden drugs to cure or control specific ailments, the root cause of which is usually never addressed.

It doesn't work.

And more and more people are getting wise to this truth. That's why it is imperative at this time that the Holistic Business Owners — those who are not bound by shareholder demands for profit above well-being — begin to really step up and expand their reach. In short: You are needed more than ever before.

The Great Awakening

People are waking up. Some are waking up to the fact that their doctors' blanket prescription for continual medication is NOT helping. Others are waking up spiritually or politically, as they come to understand that the world, as we have been told, is not what it seems.

These are the people who are having spiritual awakenings, political awakenings, near death experiences or tragedies in their lives — events and circumstances that shock them into seeing the world differently.

Spirit, Mind and Money

And all of these people need YOU.

As we roll into our new Age of Aquarius, more and more people are waking up and are looking for answers. They are looking for YOU.

Thanks to the internet, they can find you no matter where they are or where you are. Yet they can only find you if you know how to utilize this powerful tool. And that's another place where many of us get stuck. How can we be available for *them* if we don't step up to the new tools available to *us*?

What I am finding is that Holistic Business Owners are all over the map when it comes to tech skills and internet savvy. Yet most, beyond a poorly planned website that does nothing for them, have little else when it comes to real reach.

If I were a betting woman, I'd say that most business owners now have their own websites. Unfortunately, with billions of web pages on the world wide web, that doesn't mean much at all. It's like having your number listed by your last name in the New York City white pages: Highly unlikely *anyone* will ever find you!

Today, it takes a *lot* more than just a website to reach the folks who are looking for you — the ones who need and want your services. The good news is: It's not all that difficult, if you get the right kind of guidance. The guidance you will find in the pages of this book.

Fear, Power, and Your Business

And this leads us to the fear and power quote with which I began the book.. What do Fear and Power have to do with your business?

A lot!

Since that fateful day in September, 2001, there's been a proactive and highly strategic roll-out of control across the western world.

15

Guised in the form of Patriotism, Security and Terrorist Threat, this roll-out has a clear agenda of *control-through-fear*.

And while many of us see through the BS, we are not immune to the fear because it's hitting us where we live ... our material security. Fast-forward to 2008 and the one-two economic blow knocked down even those of us who weren't cringing.

The losses were staggering. The recovery is not what we had hoped. The ones hit hardest may have had a lot to lose to begin with, but that's impacted all of us — whether we had a business then or plan to start one now.

Fear is everywhere. It's a fire that's ripped through even the most seemingly impervious communities because our sense of security has been destabilized. For those who didn't buy into fear of terrorism, the bigger threat has bowled through our door: homelessness, hunger, the sheer terror of becoming a bag lady (or man).

అఠ

Fear is everywhere. And it's that fear that keeps us small...keeps us from taking risks... and from the conversations we need to have about money, service & success.

And it's that very fear which keeps us playing small. It keeps us from taking risks and for many Holistic Business Owners, it keeps us from the conversations we need to have — and the decisions we must make — about money.

Because no matter what your beliefs are about the current economic system, if you are not willing to look at money, leverage it for business growth and yes, for personal wealth, then you stand a very good chance of being rolled right under by the economic shifts that put more money in the hands of business owners, companies and corporations, and far less in the hands of employees.

To Be a Holistic Business Owner Today

For those who have lead the way in the different arenas of the Great Awakening— from activists like Starhawk who vocalized resistance to nuclear armament, to the courageous organic farmers, midwives, feminists, energy workers and yoginis ... to the folks like you and me who refused to buy-in to society's demand for our sleepy-headed conformity ... to the front-line way-showers, the mavericks and trail blazers who follow an inner conviction despite the fear that sometimes arises: The Power of our vision, our conviction, our Spirit, is *usually* stronger than our fear.

Thanks to those early trailblazers, today we have an entire economy — a legion of people — living a holistic lifestyle. If you are reading this, you are one of them. And if you want to serve them, through the entity of a business, you cannot allow the climate of fear that has now run rampant in our world control you. Instead, YOU have to take control of your business and your inner conversation around money. When you do, it can change your life, your business and your ability to help others. It did for me, and for many others I know. In Part III you'll find plenty of talking points to facilitate this conversation.

How to Use This Book

There are four parts to this book. Each has a very different focus. Together they make up what amounts to a new Conversation, one designed to support Holistic Business Owners in growing healthy, sustainable, *successful* businesses. Each section of this book includes specific exercises you can to do in order to gain clarity, build a plan, take action or evaluate ideas and beliefs that may not be serving you.

All of the exercises can also be downloaded from my website. Together, they make a great workbook to accompany this book.

Part I: Spirit

In Part I, we begin with a look at the Spirit of your Business. In this section you will discover why your Brand Message is critical and why so many Holistic Business Owners drop the ball on this, defaulting to *modality-speak* and trying to serve everybody. We'll also have a look at what it takes to create an Ideal Client profile, and why it's so important to talk about that four-letter-word: *pain*.

Part II: Mind

Part II focuses on the Mind of your Business.* This is the "manual" portion of the book, and is designed as a reference guide. Part II includes plenty of take-a-ways for building and marketing your business — both online and off. The best way to use it is to implement one or two things at a time, rather than feeling as if you need to apply all the suggestions at once. (In fact, please *don't* try that! It will only lead to overwhelm and discouragement.) Instead, keep the book in your office after you've read it through, so that these strategies are always at your fingertips!

* Even though it comprises the second part of this book, if you are new to, or uncomfortable with marketing, you can choose to skip this section, read Parts III and IV first, then return to it when you are ready to take business-building actions.

Part III: Money

Part III demands your courage. Remember when I talked about the "Heart" of a fighter? Part III is when you will need it. This is when we slay some sacred cows around money generally, and as it relates to business service and success. So if you have struggled financially as you attempt to turn your soul purpose or calling into a genuine living, this will quite probably be the least appealing part of the book for you. But it will also be the most important, because without it, no other business vision, hopes, strategies or tactics will help you.

Part IV: A New Conversation

Part IV is where we get you set up to thrive as a Holistic Business Owner. This is where we look at how to reframe outdated ideas about money, elevate your ability to have more money, provide great service and enjoy success. I also touch on my own story from struggle to success in Part IV. I share details about the important role that sub-conscious reprogramming played in healing my own Money Conversation, and how that served to propel me to where I am today.

Now ... Let's begin!

PART 1: SPIRIT

The Spirit of your Business is the heart of your business. It's your love, your purpose, your calling. It's your reason and motivation, as well as your actual work.

Whether it's some kind of service, product, program or training doesn't matter when it comes to the Spirit of your Business. What matters is that you are uniquely suited to do this work and it has meaning for you on a soul level.

Yet the Spirit of your Business is more than that. It's also how you communicate what it is you have to offer. In the world of marketing, this is called your Brand Message, and in this section, we're going to look at what it means to communicate your message clearly — and to the right audience.

That may sound simple, but it's actually one of the places where many Holistic Business Owners fall flat. We may be very clear about who we are and what we do, but when it comes to *communicating* that value in a powerful, compelling way, we sometimes make one very big mistake.

Let's have a look at exactly what this mistake is, so that if you are making it too, we can get you back on track.

Chapter One
Communicating the Spirit of Your Business

You know the purpose and value of what you do. You've got the certifications, the education, the experience, and the desire. You know your business is capable of providing valuable benefits and transformation to others. You know you can help.

Now you have to get clear on *communicating* that value with a message that grabs the attention and resonates with the people you most want to serve.

That's why, to build a business that serves, it must have a clear message and promise. Makes sense, right? But here's the sticking spot for a lot of people: Your message needs to speak to your "Ideal Client."

"But Dawn," (I hear, often) "I want to help anyone I can. I don't have an *ideal* client!"

I understand. There's a lot of confusion about this concept of an "Ideal Client." After all, many of us can and do work with a wide variety of people — people whose demographic profiles run a wide spectrum. But when it comes to your *Ideal* Client, it's not demographics that you need to look at. It's something else entirely.

Now, before we look specifically at how to clarify your Ideal Client, the first thing we need to do is have a look at the trap many of us fall into when we are not trained to speak the Spirit of our Business in a way that actually grabs people's attention.

Beware of *Modality-Speak!*

When we don't know how to communicate the value of our offering, or we are trying to speak to everyone, we often fall into what I call Modality-Speak. Modality-Speak is when, rather than communicating directly to a specific client or customer's needs, we talk about what we do: our expertise or certificates, how much we want to help, how much we can help, and ... our modalities.

The example below is drawn from several different websites. While you won't find these exact words on any one site, they represent a common approach to Home Page content. It's an approach used by many Healers and Therapists who haven't carefully developed their message so that it "speaks" to their Ideal Client.

"My name is Lorena Michele So-and-So, and I am a [insert professional title] who is deeply committed to assisting my clients on their path to physical and emotional wellbeing.

I strive to provide my clients with professional skills, empathy and understanding that will help them transition towards healing.

I am here to assist you with both [expert modality #1] as well as various alternative healing modalities.

I believe that the power of healing is innate within the human psyche, and anyone can achieve it by making a commitment to it, and seeking professional support.

I firmly adhere to the client driven model which is based in the understanding that clients always have a voice in determining their true needs.

My specialty, [expert modality #1] with an emphasis in [another modality] has lead to exciting breakthroughs with clients. I am also certified in [insert several more modalities.]

Did this message speak to you? Did it compel you to want to know more? Did you feel like your needs, concerns, fears, or pain were immediately acknowledged? *Could you even get through it?*

Probably not. Why? Because it's all about the practitioner, and has nothing whatsoever to do with the readers' pain, needs, or solution they seek.

Sure, Lorena Michele So-and-So was expressing her care, concern, sincerity, and authenticity. The trouble is, she wasn't "speaking" to the needs of the people she *could* be helping!

Here's What You Want to Remember

The problem with the kind of communication shown above is that it's meaningless to people looking for help. Why? Because no matter how good people are, they are concerned first with their own problem. So you need to be able to tell them immediately that you understand THEIR problem and have the solution they are looking for.

In other words, when someone is up at 3 a.m. because they are sick and tired of living in anxiety, and their medications don't do anything but exhaust them, they don't want to know about your credentials or your heartfelt ideals for helping. They just want to know if you can help them find relief from anxiety.

Answer These Three Questions First

Your written material, website, talks, presentations and videos, should quickly answer three questions for your audience, right off the bat:

1. What is it?
2. Who is it for?
3. What's in it for me (WIIFM)?

This is why communicating the Spirit of your business is about explaining the *transformation* you offer, and doing it in a way that is meaningful to the people you can help. In a way *they* can hear it.

How do you do that? By building a profile of your Ideal Client. Feeling uncertain about this? That's okay. I'm going to walk you through it.

There are at least two reasons why you need to clarify an Ideal Client *before* you begin any kind of business messaging, marketing or advertising:

1. Profiling your ideal client is an exercise in specificity for YOU, not exclusivity for them. In other words, it's an exercise – a necessity, really – for your own clarity.
2. The number of people you can powerfully attract is directly, *inversely*, proportional to the degree of specificity you have about your Ideal Client.

Here's why this works. The more clearly you have in your mind's eye exactly who you are communicating to, the easier, more honest, authentic, and clear your business and message will be. It helps prevent you from watering down your message.

Specifying your ideal client has nothing to do with excluding certain people from your products or services. There may well be people who will self-select as *not* being a match for you, but this is what you want. Why bother trying to attract folks you can't serve or who don't relate to you?

Almost every single client I work with starts with resistance to narrowing their Ideal Client. Even when my above argument makes sense to them, they can't figure out how to narrow down who this imaginary, Ideal Client might be.

Maybe you feel this way too. Here's why: You're probably thinking demographically. But when it comes to Ideal Clients, demographics are often irrelevant.

Instead, we have to look to the common denominator ...

Chapter Two
Pain is the Doorway to Solution

Let's Talk About Pain

Eww, pain. Who wants to talk about *that?* Well, I do. And, I want you to talk about it too. If you are a physical healer or practitioner of some sort, this won't be too difficult. If, however, your work is more along the lines of inspiring, guiding, mentoring, or uplifting others, you may feel understandably more resistance here.

So here's what you want to know. Until you can get to the bottom of what the common denominator problem, trouble, obstacle or pain is for the people you most want to serve, you will never be able to help as many people as you can.

Please understand that when I use the word "pain" in this context, I don't necessarily mean misery and suffering. What I mean is that each person you are ideally suited to help and serve is looking for a solution to something. It could be as simple as: "I need some pampering with a good massage," or it could be the need to find a trustworthy service provider, like a great dentist who doesn't use mercury for fillings, or the right home water purification system.

Whatever it is you do, when people are looking for you, they're looking for a solution of some kind. So when we look at communicating the Spirit — and the *value* — of your business, we want to come at it from the perspective of that person *looking for* what you've got.

And when they're looking, it's because they're motivated to find a solution to a problem — even when that problem isn't exactly painful.

When the Law of Attraction Doesn't Work

A former client of mine had a lot of resistance to looking at the pain points as part of clarifying his Business's Brand Message. He is a published author and teacher of Law of Attraction skills. When we first began working together, Juan was enthusiastic and ready to help a LOT of people. He had devoted a number of years to writing and then publishing his book, and really wanted to make a big impact in his community and the world.

Juan had lived a very happy life for the most part. He was blessed with what we would call good fortune on many levels: love, health, finances, relationships. He loved being able to help others experience some of the *joie de vivre* that came so naturally to him by teaching the principles, skills and exercises of the Law of Attraction. The challenge though, was that he wasn't reaching as many people as he had hoped. In fact, he was hardly reaching *anyone* and wasn't making any money on his book or his classes. So when he came to me, he had a great deal of knowledge and expertise. But his lack of reach meant he was spending his retirement funds on a fantasy business.

We mapped out some plans of where he could optimize his reach locally, and then had a look at building his Brand Message.

This is where Juan's resistance showed up. For him, looking at the pain of his ideal students was antithetical to the very principles he was teaching. He simply wanted to "attract the people who felt drawn to the work."

That's all well and good when you're Esther Hicks and have numerous New York Times Best-Sellers, happen to be the channel for a wisdom teacher called Abraham, and have a Best-Seller with the compelling title *Ask and it is Given.*

But when you are unknown in a market now *flooded* with Law of Attraction teachers, the chances of simply "attracting the people who resonate" are slim at best.

It was a bit like pulling teeth to help Juan realize that as long as he was unwilling to explore the kinds of pain people were in when they sought his guidance, he would have very few takers indeed.

Think about it. People don't lay awake in the middle of the night thinking things like: "Gee, I *really* need to raise my vibration so I can enhance my spirituality" or "if I could only find the right business mentor, my life would be perfect!"

More likely, they're up at 3 a.m. engulfed with the frustration, doubt, uncertainty, fear or *pain* about the problem they need to solve. They're up with thoughts like: "I can't stand my life!" or "I'm fed up with this [insert pain here]!" or "I'm exhausted from working this hard and never getting anywhere with my business! What am I going to do?" or "What's it going to take to create peace with my [teen, spouse, parent, employer]?"

In other words, people start looking for help when things hurt, when a crisis hits, when a solution is urgently needed, or when negative emotion is too gripping to cope with alone.

Now, if you are struggling with this concept of focusing on the pain, first of all ... take a breath :) Second, read through the short visualization below. As you do, you'll find yourself much more able to understand why this specific focus will help you more powerfully serve your clients and customers.

... Imagine someone who would very much benefit from your service or product. Imagine them climbing from their bed in the middle of the night —their hair tussled, their eyes half closed.

31

They've been tossing and turning for awhile now, restless from their mind mulling over something. Tired, but wide awake, frustrated maybe, or worried — or both — they finally climb out of bed ...

Maybe they get a drink of water or stare blankly into the fridge for a moment. But then they head to their computer. They turn it on, pull up Google and type something in ...

What are they typing in? What are they looking for? ...

What they are typing in, is exactly what YOU are looking for! It's their pain or frustration or burning question they want answered. It's the solution they seek.

Take a moment now to turn it over in your head. Mull it around a bit yourself. What did that imaginary, sleepless person type on their keyboard? What was their frustration, worry, or concern? How can you help them with that?

Once you've given this some thought, ask yourself the following question. Are there different ways someone might express this same trouble, problem or pain?

Write down your answer..

Now, take some time to answer this question:

How can you tell them you've got what they're looking for?

Use your imagination and then write out some ways you might express this to them. Don't worry about grammar or anything right now, just focus on speaking to them about what they're going through and how you can help.

Go ahead, write down what comes to you, right now. Once you give yourself a little time to do this exercise, you'll be able to see why understanding someone's pain (struggle, obstacle, frustration, or puzzle they need to solve) is essential to your ability to *communicate the Spirit of your business.*

Your First Touch Point

Your first objective as a business owner is to express the Spirit of your business in a way that jumps off the screen, grabbing the attention of that guy or gal at 3 a.m., and then connecting with them enough for them to take action in YOUR direction. This is your Brand Message, and online or off, it's your first touch point or opportunity to make a connection.

Here's one more way to come at this. What is the obstacle you help people overcome? What's the struggle or problem you help them solve? From there, turn it around and describe what that struggle is from *their* point of view. Get detailed about the impact this struggle is having on their lives. Either way you come at it, you need to get clear on *their* pain.

Once you've got a few good ways to describe the challenges or pain that would get them looking for the kinds of products, programs, or services you offer, then (and only then) it is time to have a look at *demographics.* This is when you create a profile of your Ideal Client.

"Why do I need to do that?" you may be asking. The answer is this: The better you understand your client, the more focused your business strategy will be. For example, if your Ideal Client is university educated, then the language and information on your marketing materials should be aimed at their level of sophistication; if your client is in a low- to mid-income demographic, then it will affect your pricing policies; if they are in their twenties, chances are you'll have more luck reaching them on Twitter, than with a brochure; and if you want to do an open house or presentation, there's no use booking the community hall in the country, if your clients hang out at Starbucks in the City!

The exercises at the end of this section will help you specify some key aspects of your clients' demographics.

Tying it All Together

Let's go back to those three questions that you must answer for your client.

1. What is it?
2. Who is it for?
3. What's in it for me?

Here's an example:

What is it?	A Massage	Business Coaching
Who is it for?	People who have tight neck muscles and headaches; people who work at computers for long periods of time.	People making the leap from corporate employee to entrepreneurship.
What's in it for me?	Relief from pain so you can get a good night's sleep and you won't need to take pain killers or other unwanted medications.	Support for building a business marketing plan, learning how to sell services or structure a business for growth.

You try it now:

What is it?	wt loss	
Who is it for?	women who have tried every diet + feel obsessed w/food	
What's in it for me?		

Before moving on to the next section, I urge you to make sure that you have answers for the three questions above. Then, use the exercises below to help you get very clear about who you most want to reach and serve. When you do, all your marketing, sales and promotional efforts moving forward will prove much more effective. You will also be able to implement the strategies I share in Part II more quickly and effectively.

The first exercise includes the questions listed above so that you are certain about what the common denominator pain, obstacle, or struggle is for your Ideal Client. In exercise two, you can sketch out some of the demographic characteristics of your Ideal Client or customer. Finally, in exercise three, you tie it all together with the four-step process I take many of my own clients through when they begin working with me. I know you'll find it to be a helpful, powerful way to create a compelling message which communicates the Spirit of your business!

Once you have a clear message about the Spirit and value of your business — a message that grabs and speaks to your Ideal Client — you are ready to move on to Part II of the book: the Mind of your Business.

EXERCISE 1: Your Ideal Client's Biggest Problem

1. What problem, struggle, or obstacle is your *ideal* client urgently seeking a solution to? (Hint: What would keep them up in the night worrying or searching?)

I can never lose weight

I'm addicted to food

I'm obsessed about my body

My health is getting worse

2. What is the language *they* use to describe their problem?

over weight, fat, yo-yo diet

emotional eater

menopause

powerless hopeless

3. Are there other ways your Ideal Client might express this same problem or the solution they seek?

I want to be healthy

   "   " move more

freedom

4. What secondary issues or problems might they have which are related to the main problem?

BP, thyroid, hormones
DM, cholesterol, allergies
depression, trauma, anxiety
↓ libido

EXERCISE 2: Your Ideal Client's Demographic Profile

1. What is the age range of your Ideal Client?

    20 – 65

2. Where does your Ideal Client live (owned home, apartment, city, countryside, rental ...)?

    not in a yurt

3. Marital Status of your Ideal Client?

4. Annual Income range of your Ideal Client?

    >30,000 +

5. Education level of your Ideal Client?

    college

6. What groups, associations or memberships do they belong to?

    womens groups, business networks, church

7. What activities does your Ideal Client do for fun?

    Relate, friends, crafts

8. What does your Ideal Client read or watch on TV, or do for entertainment?

EXERCISE 3: Create Your Compelling Message!

It's time to build your compelling message. This is a four-part process that I take most of my clients through in order to help them clarify the Spirit of their business and then communicate it in a way that is compelling to the people who need them most.

Remember: whatever your industry, service or client-base, without a Compelling Message, your good work in the world will not attract clients or customers.

A **Compelling Message** comes from having crystal clarity about the following three things:

1. Your **Purpose** or Mission (Who you are and why you do what you do)
2. Your **Benefits** (What results do people get from you/your service or product?)
3. Your **Audience** (Who you serve)

In order to create your **Compelling Message**, you will want to do the following:

1. Write and re-write your **Purpose**, honing it and polishing it until it is as smooth as alabaster.
2. List every possible **Benefit** someone may get from working with you/your product.
3. Create a personality profile of at least one and up to three people who represent your ideal **Audience**.

Part 1: Your Purpose

Step 1: List as many answers to the following statement as you can: "The purpose of my business is to ...." (Be sure to do this part without "thinking" with the analytical mind. You want to be in a relaxed mental state, allow yourself to freely associate, and don't let your pen come off the page.

help women find body r soul balance

introduce them to their bodies

stop fighting their bodies

step into power

fire up their sexuality

make peace w/ body

connect to something deeper

☆ blame, shame + guilt

Step 2: Put this away for at least 24 hours.

Step 3: Reread your **Purpose** list and make changes/additions as necessary.

Step 4: Put away your **Purpose** list and move on to Part 2

Part 2: Your Benefits

Step 1: List out all the possible **Benefits** people may receive with you/your services or products.

Step 2: Research the websites of your industry's leaders. Look for the Benefits they spell out on their home page, their products page(s), their reviews by satisfied clients/customers, and any other pages on their site.

Step 3: List their **Benefits**.

Step 4: Research reviews of your industry leaders. If they have books, read the negative reviews on Amazon.com (and a few positive ones too).

Step 5: List the **Benefits** people were looking for that they did or did not receive from the book or product. What benefits did users emphasize?

Step 6: Once you've compiled a solid list of **Benefits** that your industry leaders promise, and a list of other **Benefits** their 'tribe' is looking for, compare these to your own list.

Step 7: Adjust your list according to any insights you've gained about your **Benefits**.

Part 3: Your Audience

Some people resist defining their Ideal Client, wanting to help everyone or anyone who needs it. But remember: *The more precisely you can define your Ideal Client — especially their PAIN and the SOLUTION they seek — the more clearly you will craft your message.* And when you do that ... you will attract more clients!

Step 1: Compare what you've discovered in Parts 1 and 2 with your Ideal Client.

Step 2: If you are not certain about your Ideal Client, think about the people you most enjoy spending time with, working with, and helping. They are probably in the same shoes you once were, before you stepped up to where you are now. **HINT**: If you imagine you are climbing a ladder, your Ideal Client is just two or three rungs behind you.

Step 3: Profile your Ideal Client. Give them a name, a profession, an age, marital and family status, career, and most importantly — specifically define their **PAIN** and the **SOLUTION** for which they are searching.

Part 4: Back to Purpose

Get your **Purpose** statement(s) out again and rewrite them according to your new knowledge and understanding of your **Audience**, their pain, and the solutions/**Benefits** you offer.

Compelling Message Check List

Use the checklist below to help you complete the process, noting anything you've discovered about your Ideal Clients, their pain, and how you have their solution.

Parts and Steps	Completed	Discoveries and AHAs
Part 1: Your Purpose		
Part 2: Your Benefits		
Part 3: Your Audience		
Part 4: Back to Purpose		

PART II: MIND

Welcome to Part II of *Spirit, Mind & Money!* Now, you may notice some discomfort about business strategy or marketing — perhaps you suspect that most marketing is inauthentic or fake; or a bothersome time-waster; or a bunch of false advertising techniques used by people who just want to trick innocent victims out of their money. I want to invite you into a different conversation ...

And it begins with YOU.

As we've already established, there is no better time for your services, products, or programs to be of help in the world. You are needed and, as the trend continues, what you do is likely to be in ever-increasing demand. It's simple. When you have a way to solve people's problems, what you do *matters.*

And because what you do matters, ensuring people can find you, and understand that you hold a solution they seek, is as critical for them as it is for you. This is where bringing strategy to your business and learning how to market your business effectively becomes so crucial. Here's why ...

Strategic business planning and marketing are the *vehicles* that will let you reach and serve more people in a way that supports your livelihood. And the good news is, it's totally possible to do this with both *authenticity and heart.*

You see, the new way of *authentic marketing* will help to guide the perception of who you *really* are. You just need to know what to do and how to do it. Part II of this book shows you exactly what to do and how to do it!

Before You Go Further ...

WARNING: If this section seems too technical for you right now, or if you just don't feel you are in a place to start thinking about this yet — let alone planning your business strategy and marketing — that's okay! I encourage you to move on to Parts III and IV first. Then, when you are ready to take action on business-building, come back to this portion of the book and use it as your manual and guide.

Minding Your Business

The *Mind of your Business* is your Business Plan and Strategy. This includes information that a lender will want to see, such as financials and projections, and it also includes your *strategy* for promoting your business and building a prospect and client base. This is where we build your Marketing Plan and we put on our thinking caps! In fact, highlighting, underlining, sticky-noting and margin scribbling are encouraged. :)

You'll be making important and sometimes tough decisions when you create your Business Plan and Strategy. This is because marketing and outreach requires the investment of both money and time. That's why you have to plan how you want to do this, including what, how, and when you will be investing for growth.

But before we dive in, and just to be 100% clear here, I am not qualified to advise you on finances, funding, or how you should structure your business for tax purposes. You'll want to consult with an accountant and an attorney for these important decisions. What I *am* qualified to share with you is what to consider when it comes to your Marketing and Outreach Plan. I do this in the next three chapters:

Again, A Not-Too-Dangerous Warning

First, I want to assure you that you can get through this part of the book. Even if you find marketing, strategy, and "techy stuff" rather unappealing, I've worked very hard to make sure there's no "geek-speak" overwhelm here!

And ... this part of the book does gets a bit technical in places, especially in the Online Marketing section. I've made every effort to write in plain English, and provide you with the information every business owner needs to know about marketing for success in our modern, interconnected world.

I've included a lot of educational information for you, and you'll find many suggestions and strategies for effectively reaching more people who need what you've got.

My secondary goal with Part II is to assist you in learning as you go, in case you don't know, some of the terms or unique marketing strategies that are frequently used in our new, digital age.

So then, now that you've been fairly warned (and hopefully encouraged), let's dive in, shall we?

Chapter Three
Getting Clear on the "M" Word

The "M" Word

Marketing, my dear Holistic Business Owner, is your friend. Marketing has been given a bad rap. For many authentic and heart-centered service providers, "marketing" seems like the exact opposite of being authentic. Like putting on a false face, making false-promises, or haranguing people into buying.

Perhaps because big businesses with huge marketing budgets use high technology that can airbrush *anything* into existence on a billboard, ad or website ... we're suspicious. And for good reason. But as I pointed out in the introduction to this section, there are ways to market your business which are fully authentic; ways that can help to guide the perception of who YOU really are for people. So stick with me, because you're going to discover plenty of them right here!

Too Smart for Our Own Good?

The biggest challenge I find with expert clients of all kinds is that because they are brilliant at what they do, they think they can figure out the marketing thing too. Unfortunately, that's rarely the case, and what results is often a big mess. I call it 'getting in our own way,' and it's rampant among small business owners who are bright, motivated, and self-funded.

When the mess gets too big (unwieldy websites, discombobulated messaging, too many wasteful moving parts and not enough money flowing in) marketing consultants like me get called to clean things up. Unfortunately even then, we sometimes have to wrangle with clients who insist on controlling what happens and are unwilling to follow proven strategies.

This is a big red flag for me, and I no longer take on clients who aren't "coachable" in this way, or are unwilling to implement the strategies I advise. (I'm sure you coaches out there know exactly what I mean!)

To be fair, I'm as guilty of this "getting in my own way" behavior as the next person. We all have moments of weakness or poor judgment when we try to do for ourselves what really should be outsourced to others who are better at it.

Here's an example: My skills in copywriting and marketing don't translate into great online management (like website creation, list management software and other technological things I sometimes refer to as "button-pressing hell"). But it took me a long time to figure that out. After all, I'm smart, I'm a pretty organized gal, I know how to build a basic website ... why should I pay someone to handle my website, social media, technical whiz-bangery, or design ... *right?* Wrong!

Getting in our own way wastes way too much time, energy, and ultimately, money. That's why, unless marketing is your forte, I recommend mentorship or outsourcing some support for this critical part of your business. This lets you stay focused on what you do best.

So I have a request for you: If you do not know about marketing, or even if you *do* know about marketing because you studied it in college or handled marketing for a company, or have done lots of networking ... I want you to set your expertise aside for the duration of this section of the book. It's not because your experience or knowledge doesn't have value. I ask because it may get in the way of your ability to fully take in what's working *now*; what's working *in particular* for small, solo business owners who don't have big start-up budgets; and what's working *online* in terms of marketing your business successfully. Will you accept my request?

Remember: Your high calling will not have the chance to take hold if you don't have the reach necessary to bring in the capital required to keep it going.

It's Not About Facebook

The first thing I want to share with you is that your marketing success is not about Facebook! There is a huge misconception among small business owners who are new to the internet. It goes something like this: Build a Facebook fan page and my fans will become my customers.

Nope. It's an urban legend. But let me be clear here: this doesn't mean you *shouldn't* have a Facebook fan page. And it doesn't mean that some of them won't become your customers. It just means that this formula is way too simplistic. As a stand-alone strategy, it just doesn't work.

There is much more involved in leveraging Facebook or other Social Media (Twitter, Pinterest, LinkedIn, YouTube, etc.) in order to make money through your online contacts. These channels are not stand-alone solutions. They're part of an interconnected web (couldn't resist — pun intended!) of marketing efforts, so they must be combined with things like a website, advertising, campaigns, and yes, a *strategy*.

Claro? Good!

Put Facebook and the rest aside for the moment, and let's first look at some core *offline* elements you will want in place for a solid

Marketing Plan. Once we've looked at those, we'll turn back to the World Wide Web and dive into the specifics of how you can leverage the internet to reach and serve more people.

Now ... Deep Breath Please

If any of this sounds unpleasant, let's just begin with a nice, deep breath. Ahhhhhh ...

I encourage you to stick with me here because I know you'll get a lot out of what you're going to discover. In fact, I'm sure it won't be unpleasant at all, because I am going to show you:

- Exactly which steps to take and in which order
- What to do, what not to do
- What you MOST need to effectively promote and build your business

Chapter Four
Offline Marketing: Six Strategies for Success

Going Old School — Traditional Marketing isn't Dead!

The good news — for those of us born before 1990 — is that not all marketing strategy needs to be online. Nor should it be! Unless you are a full-fledged, internet business, the old school ways of marketing will still reach your ideal clients and customers.

In this chapter, we'll cover six offline marketing strategies you will definitely want to employ at different points in the growth of your business. These are proven strategies to help you get in front of the people who are looking for what you've got.

They are:

1. Networking
2. Advertising
3. Snail Mail
4. Booths & Sponsorships
5. The 100 Lb Phone
6. Speaking

Offline Marketing #1:
Networking — Like Dating Only Different

Networking can be a real challenge for many of us. If you are a natural introvert, you already know what I'm talking about! All those people, seeming so confident, well-dressed and self-assured ... you might ask yourself things like: "What have I got to offer here?" or "how can I compete with these professional looking people?" or "*jeeze!* Everyone is already clumped in groups and talking! I feel like a dork just standing here by myself ... I think I'll leave."

ℰℭ

When it comes to Networking, you want to focus on being of service and being a connector rather than a hunter.

ℰℭ

I know. I've been there. Many of us have. And even though I am not really an introvert, I'm not a super-extroverted type either. In fact, I literally had to *learn how* to "chit-chat" in social settings. After all, my social life had been forged during sacred ceremonial circles, academic feminist seminars, and later (in of all places), a martial arts gym.

These were a world away from the "booze-n-schmooze" cocktail hours I had to frequent as journalist, or the business networking luncheons I now attend from time to time.

Like many of you who may be reading this, networking was not my idea of a good time. I would often find myself coming up with excuses for avoiding these valuable opportunities to connect with community influencers. Ultimately, my avoidance did not serve me or my business.

The truth is, few of us are born networkers. We have to learn the social etiquette of it as well as the skills for meeting new and different people. This can be especially challenging for the Holistic Business Owner when networking with folks who may have radically different values than we do. But despite these differences, it *is* possible to network effectively, and build alliances, contacts, and prospects for your business.

I learned the foundational elements of effective networking from Joe Sweeney in his book, *Networking is a Contact Sport.*[2] Sweeney is very much an old school businessman, and while he and I would probably have little, if anything to talk about at a dinner party (except maybe boxing), I always appreciate solid business wisdom from my elders — especially when they're highly successful. In *Networking*, Sweeney offers many examples of how to build contacts for business. But the biggest take away for me was this: Your focus when networking is to be of service.

"Hi, My Name is Dawn. Do You Want to Make Out?"

I like to compare networking with dating. If you met someone for the first time and you liked them, would you say: "Hi, my name is Dawn, do you want to make out?" Probably not.

You'd probably take some time to get to know them. You'd ask them questions. You'd get curious. You'd listen more than you spoke. Only if you detected a mutual interest or attraction would you then want to invite them on a more personal "date." Maybe you'd ask them for a cup of coffee, or to join a few others for dinner, a movie or an outing. In time, you'd get to know each other better, and a more romantic date might be in order. Maybe even a kiss. And so it goes.

---

[2] Sweeney, Joseph. *Networking is a Contact Sport: How Staying Connected and Serving Others Will Help You Grow Your Business, Expand Your Influence - or Even Land Your Next Job.* BenBella Books, Inc. Dallas, TX. 2010.

When you go to a networking event and start passing out your business cards without taking the time to get to know someone, it's kind of like saying: "Hi, my name is Dawn, do you wanna make out?" *Ewww.*

Instead, choose to connect. Listen more than you talk. Find out what people do, who they serve, and the prospects they would like to meet at the event you're attending, or in the future. If you can refer someone you know to them, by all means do it! Be a connector rather than a hunter.

You'll find that by approaching networking from a stance of service, more people will be of help to you. Remember, even if you walk into a room of people who are not your Ideal Clients, you might meet someone who knows someone who is your Ideal.

Be of service FIRST. This is what you want to think about when you network. When you meet someone, really *listen* to them. Listen to what their business is, what their needs and interests are, and who they might be looking to connect with as a prospect or service provider.

Instead of seeing them as either a potential customer or not, see them as a potential *collaborator* — someone with whom you may be able to refer business in the future. When you approach networking in this way, you will find that "what goes around, comes around" and in time, those you meet will begin to refer people to you.

eWomen Network – A Stellar Model for Smart Networking

I am a member of eWomen Network* and their model for networking is fantastic. In fact, whether you are a woman or a man, if you serve female clientele, I highly recommend you attend an eWomen networking event in your area.

During each monthly Accelerated Networking Luncheon, before we eat, we gather in circles of about 6-10 people.

Each person has 60 seconds to share their name, their business, who they are looking to meet and what they plan to purchase or invest in within the next 30-60 days.

Then, anyone who either wants that person's services, knows someone who wants their services, or has the help or resources they need, jots a note on the back of their business card and hands it to them.

There is never any passing around of unwanted business cards or foisting offers on unsuspecting victims at an eWomen event.

eWomen Network is currently in the USA, Canada and a small handful of other nations. Whether you are a woman or a smart man, I recommend you look for a local chapter and attend a luncheon. If nothing else you'll get to meet some dynamic entrepreneurial women and network in a friendly, supportive environment.

*eWomen Network: http://www.ewomennetwork.com/

A Word About Being Seen

There's an old saying: "It's not *what* you know, but *who* you know." As a Holistic Business Owner, you want to be sure to be known, particularly by the movers and shakers in your community and ideally, in your industry as a whole. That's why we network — simply to be seen. If you're the best kept secret in the marketplace, you won't be able to run a business. Networking is a way for others to get to know you, and to build that oh, so important thing in business — the "Know-Like-Trust" factor.

Offline Marketing #2:
Advertising — Mad Men Revisited

I am not a "Mad Man" (or woman) and advertising is not my expertise. Still, a great ad campaign might be a good fit for you, depending on your business. So while this section is by necessity a short one, in it we'll review a few things you'll want to consider for *offline* advertising.

Good News!

The good news about advertising is that the old days of spending a fortune on yellow pages and magazine ads are over. Yes, you still have to spend money on traditional advertising, but with the competition of the internet, it is not nearly what it once was!

I cannot speak to billboards or radio, and I would suspect TV ads are just as pricey as they've always been, but print media now faces stiff competition from the internet for your advertising dollars.

As this book goes to press, internet advertising is a multi-billion dollar industry. And without the expenses involved in print ads, there are online advertising options for every budget.

Still, there's a place for offline advertising. So if you have a business which is ideally suited for a specific print media (like your local health food store's free magazine, for example, or your community newspaper, or a professional journal), by all means consider these! Do some research into what that periodical's reach is, whether their demographics are in fact, your Ideal Clients, and of course, how much it costs. Many publications will also offer packages with online ads as well, so be sure to ask their ad reps about these kinds of offers.

As with any business marketing, be sure your ads follow sound, copywriting principles that catch the eye of readers, then immediately tell them the key benefits they will get from doing business with you.

Offline Marketing #3:
Direct Mail — What's Old is New Again

With the rampant disease called "inbox overload" affecting millions worldwide, there's been a return to direct mail as a marketing strategy. If this surprises you, just think about your own life. How many emails are in your email inbox right now? How many of them are unopened? Of the unopened emails, how many have been there for more than 24 hours? Two days? A week? More than a week?

As of this writing, inbox overwhelm still afflicts many — including many of the folks you want to communicate with. According to PandoDaily, a blog site dedicated to startup company topics, "there's an 80 percent chance that any given inbox will have between 72 and 21,000 items."[3] According to their research, the average email user has about 8,027 emails and 37 folders.

That's an awful lot of mail for even the most fastidious to manage. So when it comes to using email as a form of marketing to your ideal prospects, the competition is stiff.

By contrast, think about the last time you got a friendly postcard or letter in the mail. Not a bill or a credit card solicitation, but a semi-personalized card or note. You opened it, didn't you? (And if you're old enough to remember the pre-internet days, you probably remember tossing those friendly postcards from local business in the "circular file" before even giving them a second glance!)

---

[3] http://pando.com/2013/04/05/the-truth-about-email-whats-a-normal-inbox/

Here's an interesting fact: According to the Direct Mail Association (DMA)'s 2013 fact book,[4] 65% of consumers in all age groups made a purchase as a result of a piece of direct mail.

In marketing as with fashion, what was old occasionally becomes new again, once people get tired of the current trend.

Now, in order to use direct mail effectively, you're going to have to do your homework. Sending print materials costs money after all. And even though there are direct mail marketing services to help you cut costs, you still want to be strategic about whom you send mail to. Consider carefully whether these are actually ideal prospects, or whether they are long shots.

You also want to consider your purpose in sending a piece of direct mail. For example, if you plan to hold an event of some kind in your State's largest city, you may want to plan out a campaign with between three and nine different post cards, sent to specific zip codes which are close to the event location, and the likely demographics of people who would attend.

Another way to use postcards is to retarget people who have been following you online, used your services or shopped at your store. When you have a special event or promotion, instead of mailing postcards to your entire town, why not send them to specific people?

Offline Marketing #4:
Booths and Sponsorships — Expert Without the Limelight

Investing in a sponsorship booth at events which attract your ideal audience is a great way to get exposure. Hosting a booth can position you as an expert. It also gives you the opportunity to have conversa-

---

[4] http://www.onlinemarketinginstitute.org/blog/2013/06/why-direct-mail-still-yields-the-lowest-cost-per-lead-and-highest-conversion-rate/

tions with prospects, without having to be in the limelight of speaking at the event.

If you are not a public speaking kind of person (the #1 fear among most people), then booth sponsorships are worth considering.

A few things to keep in mind when it comes to sponsoring a booth:

- **Be available for passers-by.** Not everyone will want to visit with or talk to you, but you don't want to sit behind your table with your nose in your smart phone or a book! Get out in front of your booth. Smile, say hi, and be willing to engage with those who are interested.

- **Listen.** Just like with networking, you want to be sure to listen first — and be curious about — your booth visitor. Why are they there? What are their interests?

- **Offer a free give-away.** There are many different small gifts you can give to booth visitors. I like to give away small elephants made of cloth and attached to a key chain. I attach my business card to the keychain loop and people just love them! But see what suits your business brand, and be sure to have your business name, contact information, website and logo printed on each one.

- **Hold a raffle** and collect business cards. This is a great way to have leads for follow-up once the conference or event is over.

- **Follow-up.** All the leads in the world will do you no good if you don't FOLLOW-UP. Be sure to reach out to each and every contact, by email first, with a personalized "Nice to meet you," then follow-up by phone. Follow-up is the secret sauce to any kind of booth or sponsorship. Neglect this and you might as well have skipped the booth altogether!

Offline Marketing #5:
The 100 lb. Phone

Why "100 pounds?" Because anyone who has done cold calling for sales will tell you that the phone has got to be at least that weight every time they pick it up!

Seriously though, when it comes to growing your business, your phone is your friend. Use it often because it is the one strategy you could and should turn to every single business day until you have too many clients to find time for this important, daily routine. And even then, even when you do have plenty of clients and prospects, you still want to be sure to include the beloved, (if sometimes weighty) telephone as a part of your weekly, offline marketing plan.

Now, before you toss this book across the room please, let me clarify. I don't mean calling complete strangers. Sometimes this may indeed be the case, particularly if you've recently opened a business in town and need to get customers walking through your door. But for many of us, we are actually calling *warm* leads. These may be people we have met at networking events; people who have been referred to us by others; or people with whom we have had a brief conversation somewhere.

Picking up the phone is an essential part of your business outreach strategy, no matter how sophisticated your online marketing, and no matter how many clients or prospects you have.

But I Don't Know What to Say!

What do you say on these calls? That depends on the nature of your business. For most of you this will be an invitation for them to try out your services, take advantage of a special offer, or schedule a free session to explore their needs and your services (often called a Strategy or a Needs Discovery session).

Eventually, these calls will also include the *sales conversation*. I cover the Sales Conversation in Part III of this book, when we look at the Money component. So for now, you want to think about the following:

✓ Who are my warm leads right now?

✓ Where can I get more warm leads? (Referrals from friends, networking events, sponsoring a booth at an event where my Ideal Clients will be, etc.)

✓ What reason do I have to call these warm leads? (Invitation to a strategy session, special offer, etc.)

✓ Do I have a free offer of some kind?

✓ Do I want to invite them to schedule a conversation about their needs?

✓ Do I want to ask them what their needs are right on that first call?

✓ How can I keep track of my warm leads and keep following up with those who stay warm?

✓ Do I want to keep everyone on a spread sheet or in a note book?

✓ Shall I put notes on their business cards?

Once you've got some clarity around how you will handle your phone routine, it's time to, yeah ... pick it up.

Offline Marketing #6:
Speak Your Way to More Business

If you really want to connect with the right people — people who need what you've got and are willing to invest in getting it — probably the single best, offline marketing strategy you can use is public speaking. That's right, get up and talk about what you do!

Speaking serves to position you as an expert in your field. In fact, this is such an effective business builder that I strongly encourage you to start speaking, whatever your business. And if YOU are your brand (in other words, you provide the services directly to the client), then speaking can radically increase your reach and your success.

This doesn't mean you have to become a professional speaker, or create a big event as your speaking platform. There are plenty of opportunities for you to speak — from networking events to special focused seminars, local groups and organizations, local symposiums, or even your public library. Speaking is an opportunity you should not miss if you've got something of value to share with your community.

How to Find Speaking Opportunities

To find speaking opportunities near you is simple. All you need to do is look up some local organizations such as Chambers of Commerce, Lions Clubs, health food stores, associations, or networking groups.

Put together a short list for starters, and simply call them up and say, "Hi, do you take speakers?" If the answer is no, simply thank them and move on. If the answer is yes, then you ask them how they'd like to receive a speaking proposal, then follow up accordingly.

Pretty painless.

Engage, Educate, Entertain — Preparing a Great Talk

Preparing a great talk is an art form in itself. You want to *engage*, *educate*, and *entertain* all within one presentation. A great talk is directly connected with the strategies a copywriter employs to write engaging content that influences people to take action or form an opinion (this is called copywriting or just "copy").

That's because, just like written marketing material, a great talk is meant to *influence*. And whether that influence is related to motivating, educating, selling, or simply interesting people enough so they continue to pay attention, the fact is that you will have to keep them engaged and compelled to do it.

What Should I Say?

Ah, now we get to the challenging part! About what should you speak? There are many great books on how to write and deliver a compelling talk, but that is beyond the scope of this book. However, let's have a look at some of the factors you'll want to consider when composing a great talk.

To plan your talk, you want to be clear about your audience's needs and interests, relative to your expertise. From there, you'll want to consider length of time allotted for your talk and the level of knowledge your audience has about your topic.

For example, if you are a Personal Trainer and Fitness Expert, and you are going to be speaking about fitness to your city's local Benevolent and Protective Order of Elks (BPOE) Chapter, you may want to tailor it toward some of the specific concerns of aging members who don't get as much exercise as they should. But if you are speaking at an event tailored to parents with athletically gifted kids aiming for Olympic level competition, you will want to tailor it more toward something like physical stress factors in adolescent athletes.

To PowerPoint or Not to PowerPoint

Some of the greatest speakers of all time did not have the luxury of using a PowerPoint presentation. They relied on excellent memorization and good old fashioned charisma to engage, educate, and entertain their audiences. Even today, the stellar names in the realm of Public Speaking generally command a stage without any screen of bullet points behind them.

This being said, PowerPoint presentations do have several advantages. They work particularly well if:

* You are first starting out. This is because PowerPoint can help you to stay on track with your talk. When you handle it right, you'll also find that it will be a "touchstone" to keep you energetically grounded.

* Your talk has an educational focus. The benefit of a slide show is that when people both hear and see information, they retain it much better. (A study done by the University of Texas[5] found that people remember 10 percent of what they read, 20 percent of what they hear, 30 percent of what they see and 50 percent of what they see and hear.) For example, one of my talks is called *"Is your*

---

[5] (Metcalf 1997) found in Yahoo Answers:
https://answers.yahoo.com/question/index?qid=20061229192515AAHEEB0

Website Cashing In?" During this talk, I share with my audience three big mistakes a lot of people make with their website — mistakes that waste their money and their visitor's time. Because this is an educational talk, I use a PowerPoint presentation. But I have another presentation I do at small gatherings that involves guided imagery, inspiration, and sharing. No PowerPoint needed.

- You don't need to be a comedian, but you want to add some humor to your presentation. It's a great idea to include pictures in your slides. Funny images can work well as long as they serve to both illustrate your point and, to some degree, add entertainment value while expressing a bit of your personality.

The downside of using a PowerPoint presentation is the risk of "hiding" behind your slides. Please don't do this. You also want to avoid making your slides text-laden and then reading them like an unmemorized script. Ugh! Super boring for your audience and stressful for you. Ideally you should memorize your talk to the point that you can free-flow enough to really connect with your audience, without going so far off-topic that you lose yourself (or them).

A slide or PowerPoint presentation cannot and should not replace a great talk. You want to think of it as a supplement. It's your personal charisma and the way you deliver your talk that will keep your audience engaged.

Offline Marketing Summed Up

There are, of course, other ways to market and promote your business offline. Guerrilla marketing (unconventional and low-cost means of getting lots of exposure) can be great for events, especially in small towns. Newspaper ads and requesting referrals or giving current clients incentives to bring you new leads are all possibilities.

The best advice is to try one offline strategy at a time and do it well for 90 days. Assess it, modify it, and then introduce another offline strategy to your marketing portfolio to further enhance your efforts.

Since different businesses serve different clientele, there is no single perfect combination of offline marketing strategies for everyone. You can't afford to ignore any of them, because each will and can serve your business. Your job is to determine which of them gives you the best Return on Investment (ROI) without overwhelming you or draining you of time and money. This is why taking a step-by-step approach is best.

And now, on to the virtual arena!

Chapter Five
Online Marketing: Your Five Must-Haves

Going Virtual For Marketing Success

Online Marketing is a whole new animal for many of us who weren't born into the internet era. For those who don't spend a great deal of time online, it can be confusing and stressful to even contemplate using the internet for business. And like everything else online, marketing resources and strategies for this strange new world are many, varied, and quite sophisticated.

This section will provide you with five essential online marketing strategies:

1. Your Website
2. SEO – Search Engine Optimization
3. Social Media
4. Expert Positioning Online
5. Advertising

Plus you'll also get a great deal of support material on how to use the internet for:

- Greater reach
- To serve more people
- To make more money

You have my full permission to make this section a dog-eared mess! I encourage you to go through it with your favorite pens, highlighters, sticky notes, and even a notebook. What you'll find here is a treasure trove of marketing insights that are specific to the online world. So take a deep breath ... and let's dive in!

A Word About Technology

As a copywriter and marketing consultant, helping my clients leverage the internet is one of the primary ways that I offer support. And while we also focus on their *offline* efforts, it is the online piece that can take people down wasteful, unproductive rabbit holes all too quickly, if they don't follow sound guidance.

This is caused, in part, because most of us were not raised in the era of computers — let alone the worldwide web. When we don't have internet skills, we have a tendency to do one of two things ... avoid the internet for business all together; or waste tons of time gathering limited, free advice, then taking the wrong steps in the wrong order. Ultimately of course, this wastes precious time and money, which is why you'll want to pay close attention to what I share with you about each of these 5 strategies.

Online Marketing #1: Your Website

When it comes to building an online presence for your business, the one thing I want you to remember is this — "Build It and They Will Come" is the tagline for a movie ... *not* a marketing strategy!

One of the biggest traps I see otherwise smart business owners fall into is that they build a website and then leave it there. They don't make any effort to do the things necessary to actually have their website work for them. This is understandable, considering the fact that most of us grew up with the Yellow Pages as our only real option for advertising. So we end up approaching our website in the same way. We plunk it up there and leave it.

You want to be sure that you do more than simply put up a website and ignore it. Many new business owners start off with great intentions to launch a website. They may even get a few pages of basic content up and running, but then with the other priorities of business ownership demanding more time, the website suffers, pages remain eternally "under construction," and would-be customers get tired of checking back to pages that are never updated. You might as well hang a "Closed" sign on your business door.

Your website is the essential component of all online marketing efforts. Without one that is frequently used, modified and updated, monitored and *working for you*, you've got no way of:

- Establishing your brand and Brand Message.
- Being seen in a crowded marketplace — whatever your business.
- Ranking high on organic search results ("Google" searches).
- Getting visitors.
- Adding value to your visitors.
- Collecting leads and prospects.
- Selling stuff!

Exactly what you decide to put on your website is up to you, but some of the basics which should be included are:

1. Well thought out, compelling copywriting.
2. A Lead Magnet (explained below).
3. A way to follow-up and build relationships with people who visit your site.
4. Specific information and phrases your ideal prospects are using when they search online.
5. A blogging strategy for adding fresh content regularly.
6. A social media integration plan.
7. New pictures and videos from time to time.
8. Fresh testimonials.
9. Upgrades as needed.

At the very least, you need three key pages:

1. A Home Page
2. An About Page
3. A Sales Page (for a launch or promotion)

A Word About Split-Testing

We're going to do a little tech tangent here, because it's important for our overall conversation about online marketing. It's something called "split testing" and it's a powerful tool for your online marketing efforts. Why? Because when you employ a consistent split-testing strategy, you can get so precise about the value of your marketing efforts, that you will never again have to wonder whether your advertising dollars are working.

The concept of split testing is quite simple: Try two different things and see which one works best. Then nix the loser and retest the winner. Let's see how this might apply to, say an email, you send out ...

Write the exact same email but have two different subject lines. Let's say you have a list of 1000 people. Send the email with Subject line "A" to a random selection of 500 people, and send the email with Subject like "B" to the other 500. Then (using a list management service) check to see what the open rate was for each of the subject lines. The one with the highest rate is the winner.

The concept of split testing (also known as A-B Testing), is quite simple, but its application can be complex. There are hundreds of things you can split test in order to optimize (improve) your results online. Here are a few that most of us, at some point, will want to try:

1. Home Page Headlines
2. Sales Page Headlines
3. Email Subject Lines
4. Email Calls to Action (CTAs)
5. Guarantees
6. Sales Page Images
7. Facebook Advertising
8. Google Advertising
9. Images for Ads

Don't worry right now about how the heck to do these things. They're still a bit in your future if you are new to online marketing. The important thing here is for you to understand that marketing and advertising online gives you marketing power and insight that you've never had before. Ultimately, this power can both save you money and actually *reach more of the people you most want to serve.*

Your Website is Not the Great American Novel

The first thing you must know about your website is that you have just three seconds to grab someone's attention when that person lands on your website home page. Three! That's why every word and design element counts.

The second thing you want to understand about communicating online is that people don't read the same way they read a book. Unlike reading a book, where we read almost every word, people tend to "scan-n-dip" when reading online. It's like the virtual equivalent of flipping through a magazine at a doctor's office — you don't want to get all caught up in an article only to be interrupted, so you flip through. You "scan and dip."

What this means is that those who choose to write massive blocks of text on their website set themselves up to lose business ... every time!

Lest you think I exaggerate, just consider your own habits online. Go ahead, give it a try. You'll begin to notice that you too will bounce from a site as soon as you feel bogged down by words. (Kindle novels and iTunes magazines being the likely exceptions here.)

When you take into account the fact that we are bombarded by information every day online — they don't call it the information age for nothing — this "scan and dip" behavior makes sense. And even though it's a great thing to have so much information at our finger tips, let's face it, we are also living in the "information overwhelm" age. Most of us simply don't have time to wade through a bunch of information to get to a salient point. We want to find out what we need NOW!

A research paper by Ziming Liu studied reading behavior in the digital environment. Liu's findings[6] state: *"The screen-based reading behavior is characterized by more time spent on browsing and scanning, keyword spotting, one-time reading, non-linear reading, and reading more selectively, while less time is spent on in-depth reading, and concentrated reading. Decreasing sustained attention is also noted."*

Josh Dougherty,[7] in an article on the Masterworks Blog, states that 78% of readers scan digital content. While eye tracking studies that use heat maps to uncover reader habits recommend website owners "plan for scanning behavior."[8]

And it makes sense that people are more likely to scan. When you consider the sheer *volume* of content we are exposed to daily, it's almost mind-boggling. The website, Internet Live Stats[9] tracks well, live stats. As I write this in early 2015, the total number of websites on the world wide web is 1,169,216,804. Yes, that's 1.16 *billion*. Oh wait ... now it's 1,169,217,295 ... and counting!

There has also been 185.4 *billion* emails sent (so far) today; 3.55 *billion* Google searches today; 3,264,000+ blog posts written today; 7.12 billion YouTube videos watched; and all the social media engagement which, when added up, comes to some other exceedingly large number.

---

[6] Ziming Liu. Abstract from "Reading behavior in the digital environment: Changes in reading behavior over the past ten years." School of Library and Information Science, San Jose State University, San Jose, CA. 2005. found at: http://www.emeraldinsight.com/doi/abs/10.1108/00220410510632040

[7] Dougherty, Josh. "3 online reading behaviors you need to know about" found on http://www.masterworks.com/2011/05/3-online-reading-behaviors-you-need-to-know-about/

[8] Nielsen Norman Group. *How People Read on the Web: The Eyetracking Evidence.* Special report. Found at: http://www.nngroup.com/reports/how-people-read-web-eyetracking-evidence/

[9] http://www.internetlivestats.com/

I think you're getting the picture.

This is why the formula for writing online is very different than that of a book. It's why you will never find big long blocks of text on a decent website. And if this still isn't making sense, again I invite you to think about yourself. When was the last time you read every word of a big long email or a website laden with paragraph after paragraph of words?

Right.

So before you do anything at all with your website, it's important to understand that online, people scan more than they read. Which means it's your job to be sure what you write is compelling, easy on their eyes, and their schedules. The best way to do this is to be sure any page of your website has the following:

1. Plenty of white space
2. Short paragraphs
3. Compelling sub-heads that break the text every 2-4 paragraphs
4. Bullet points, lists, side bars, boxed-out texts or quotes

Whether you are writing a home page, free digital book or blog posts, these strategies make your website reader-friendly. And reader-friendly means your message stands a much better chance of actually being read.

Now let's have a look at exactly what you need to do in order to make the most of those three precious seconds, and grab the attention of the people who genuinely need and want what you've got.

Start with Your Home Page

Your website Home Page will be most visitor's first stop, so it's essential that you get this piece right. Far too many well intentioned website owners make a major mistake here, by trying to include *all* pertinent information about themselves and their business right on their Home Page.

Fire-hosing people with information, no matter how great that information may be, is a *serious* no-no for all but a few types of businesses. Visitors don't know where to look first or how to evaluate what's important. And when things aren't immediately clear, they leave. It's a futile form of engagement for you and too often, a frustrating experience for your website visitor.

I'm going to go over, in detail, the most important elements to include on your Home Page:

- A Feature, such as a video or audio recording, that builds the Know-Like-Trust Factor.
- The Lead Magnet offer, or free, valuable gift that addresses your visitor's pain in some way, and engages them enough to want to "opt-in" to receive it.
- A Call to Action that encourages visitors to give you their name so you can add them to your contact list and begin the Email Funnel Strategy that strives to nurture the relationship and sell your products or services.

Please understand that when people come to your site, they're not really interested in everything you have to tell them. As I shared with you in Part 1 (Communicating the Spirit of Your Business), they're really only interested in three things.

1. What is it?
2. Who is it for?
3. What's in it for me ("WIIFM")?

If you don't give them those three things immediately ... bye-bye.

How immediately? Three seconds. That's right, your website Home Page needs to answer those three questions in 3...2...1! In fact, if you don't answer the three questions that *every single person landing on your home page is secretly asing themselves*, you stand very little chance of keeping their attention.

Simple questions to answer? Yes! Easy to answer them? Not necessarily. With just three seconds, this means Clarity, Brevity, and Compelling Copywriting are essential. Let's have a look at each of these questions in turn.

Question #1: What Is It?

Remember the worksheets you did back in Part I on your Ideal Client and communicating the spirit of your business? Let's go back to the work you did there and see how you can best communicate it on your website...in three seconds!

What's Their Pain?

Looking at the work you've done, who did you identify as your Ideal Client and what answers would they be up looking for at 3 a.m.? Those first three seconds need to address the pain, struggle or obstacle people are wrangling with — that thing which motivated them to look for help on your website in the first place.

Now this doesn't mean you begin with the pain specifically, although it might! What it means is that you address it. Here are some examples of Home Page headlines which address the pain directly or indirectly:

1. You are a Business Coach and you help people get more clients.
   - ✓ "Tired of Struggling to Find your Next Client?"
   - ✓ "The Top Three Places to Find your Next Client!"
   - ✓ "How to Get More Clients Without Being 'Salesy'"

2. You are a Chiropractor and you specialize in pain relief for injury recovery.
   - ✓ "Specializing in Pain Relief from Auto and Sports Injuries."
   - ✓ "Get Back on Your Feet – Spinal Realignment to Get You Moving After Injury Knocks You Down."
   - ✓ "Relief! Chiropractic Care for Pain Relief."

3. You are a Health Coach and you specialize in weight loss.
   - ✓ "Tired of avoiding the beach every summer because you hate how you look in a bathing suit?"
   - ✓ "Lose 10 pounds ... Without Starving Yourself!"
   - ✓ "Lose Weight without Sacrificing Your Favorite Foods."

4. You are a Boutique Owner and you specialize in women's clothing.
   - ✓ "Designer Wear at Half the Price."
   - ✓ "Eclectic Styles for Women Who Want to Stand Out in a Crowd."
   - ✓ "Exclusive Designs for Discerning Taste."

You'll notice with each of these that some are speaking directly about the pain, while others are focusing more on the solution. Either way, the pain or obstacle is addressed. Jot down some ideas you have for a headline that might capture your Ideal Client.

Question #2: Who is It For?

It's important to call out to the person you are talking to somewhere near the top of your home page. This can be done in a number of ways. Often, this "call-out" comes at the very top of your page, in smaller letters, but above the major headline. It can also be at the beginning of the body copy (the web page's main content beneath the headline) in the form of a letter written directly to your specific audience. Here are a few samples:

1. If your business provides financial counseling for parents saving for their kids' college.
✓ Attention Parents: Have you Started Your Kid's College Fund Yet?
✓ Got a Middle School Student? – Grab Your College Fund Info Kit Now!
2. If you provide plumbers with a new diagnostic tool.
✓ Attention Plumbers: Time-Saving Diagnostics Adds 1000s to Your Bottom Line.
✓ For Plumbers Who Want to Save More Time and Make More Money.
3. If you offer accounting services for business coaches.
✓ For Great Coaches Who *Don't* Want to Crunch Numbers.
✓ Especially for Coaches: How to Protect Your Hard-Earned Income from the IRS!

You'll notice all of these also offer some benefit, but each speaks to a specific group of individuals. It will hook their attention and get them to read the next line. Think about a few call-outs or hooks that you could use.

Question #3: What's In It For Me (The WIIFM Factor)

Most people are good, decent folks. But this doesn't preclude them from having their own interests and concerns at the forefront of their minds, especially when they are looking for something online and have landed on your site.

This is why the WIIFM Factor is essential for your website and for all good copywriting, advertising, and talks. The WIIFM Factor is handled by providing a specific, compelling benefit. It can also include some degree of urgency in order to encourage your visitor to continue reading and to motivate them to take action, should they need what you are offering. Back in Part I, you used the worksheets to identify some of the benefits you provide. Here are some examples of how to effectively translate these benefits onto your website:

1. You are an injury attorney.
   ✓ "Know your Rights Before You Lose Your Chance for Compensation."
   ✓ "Immediate Answers when You Aren't Sure What to Do Next."

2. You are a financial planner.
   ✓ "Discover Exactly What You Need to Do NOW so You'll Never Run Out of Money."
   ✓ "Ensure Your Retirement Won't Send You to the Poor House."

3. You own a hair salon.
✓ "YOUR Style – the Way YOU Want It!"
✓ "More Than A Salon – A Boutique Experience to Pamper You the Moment You Walk in the Door!"

Can you see how each of these statements tells the reader something about what's in it for them? In these examples, of course, we haven't done an Ideal Client profile, so their effectiveness may vary — depending on the needs, frustrations, and solution the Ideal Client is seeking. (Are you beginning to see why completing the exercises at the end of Part I is so important?)

At the end of Part II, you'll be able to put together the answers to your three-second questions based specifically on your business, your Ideal Client, and the problems you solve. But before we go to those worksheets, let's move on to another key function of your website, and particularly, your website'S Home Page.

Building Rapport: The Know-Like-Trust Factor

Once you've got their attention, it's time to build rapport. I often recommend people include a video on their home page in order to introduce themselves to their visitors. This is particularly valuable if you and your service are the brand, but video for all kinds of businesses can work well. The goal is to begin to build the "Know-Like-Trust" factor.

We are all hungry these days for meaningful connection. Sure, we love the fast-paced convenience of the internet, but the truth is, many folks are lonely and they *want* to find the connections that nourish them — connections with leaders and groups they resonate with and trust.

While video is not the SAME as a live meeting, we know by the very fact of its success that it works. Video is the bridge. It's the way to make a connection and reveal your authentic self. It's a way to build rapport and trust — in you and your business.

Since the online world is the platform that can let you reach and serve countless people, we cannot discount it for its digital nature. We must leverage it, use it, soften, and enrich it. And video is one of the very best ways to do this!

This being said, I do understand that not everyone is cut out for video. Some folks just freeze up in front of a camera. They can't be natural in the same way they are in person. If you dread the camera, you can always use a slide show presentation with a voice over and picture of yourself, or even create an audio recording to begin establishing that rapport, (the "Know-Like-Trust" factor) with your website visitors.

Your List is Gold

This is something I say often to people who need help with their websites. It's essential that you capture the leads of people who visit your website in order to build said list — particularly for those who need what you've got. The point is not to get every single person's email address and first name, but to capture those who are the right prospects for you.

How NOT to Capture Leads

"The only constant is change" has never been truer than when it comes to internet marketing. Once upon a time in the early years of the internet, a few smart marketers built six and seven-figure lists. Some of them used a simple strategy called a newsletter. You've probably seen these invitations on websites: "Sign up here for our newsletter." The problem is, this strategy doesn't work the way it used to.

With a gazillion potential newsletters to choose from and a weekly dose of inbox overload for most of us, who wants another newsletter? Today, the best way to NOT build your list is by following outworn strategies like the vague promise of another newsletter. Not convinced? Ask yourself this: How many people do you imagine wake up in the morning and think (with urgency), "I need to sign up for more newsletters!"?

The bottom line is, we all have to work harder for those golden leads today, because the competition has grown and the market of prospects are more savvy.

No Farming Please

In the early days of the internet, when list management and email marketing automation was fairly new (and search engines were not very sophisticated), many people set up what amounted to "email farming" websites. They were out to capture as many email addresses as possible and then spam the crap out of them with sales-focused emails — whether these folks were a good fit for their offerings or not.

Then Google got a little more sophisticated. And a little more. And a little more. The results? Today it's not possible to simply capture any old lead. Oh, you could try. And as long as you stay under the radar of Google, you'll have some luck for awhile. But start paying for advertising and you'll eventually get caught. Besides, when you spam people they opt out and complain, so even if Google doesn't catch you, your List Management System will shut you down after too many spam complaints (see below).

Relevant and Valuable

This is good news for authentic entrepreneurs. It means that being irrelevant, scammy or spammy will not get you ahead. In fact, the great news for us is that today, it's all about relevance and value.

Thanks to Google's more advanced algorithms (a mathematical formula that evaluates the relevance and therefore, the value of any web page), in order to even get people to your site, your content has to be relevant and valuable. This helps to ensure that whatever you offer on your website as a free gift will be a good match for the people who are looking for your products or services.

From there, your list management system (for example, Mail-Chimp, ConstantContact, or more robust systems like 1ShoppingCart, InfusionSoft or Ontraport) takes over. So even if you manage to do a terrific job of attracting the right folks, capturing their lead, and then making offers to them, if you start to spam the bejesus out of them (with email after email trying to sell them stuff) your List Management System will get complaints from subscribers who select the "this is spam" button when they opt-out of your list. When a management system receives too many of these, they'll shut you down.

Again, this is great news! Because what it means is that if we do our homework, be authentic, build trust, and add value, (then combine it with some SEO (Search Engine Optimization) strategy, we can do very well indeed online!

How to Turn Website Visitors into Leads

Your best bet for turning website visitors into leads is to offer them a gift that has real value. A gift that's specific, quickly accessed, offers clear value, and is easily used. But please understand, when I say valuable, I don't mean your services. I mean a little something that gives them information or training or support, which you create once and deliver to them automatically.

These free gifts are called by different things. I refer to them most often by the name **Lead Magnet**, but here are a few names you might run across:

"Opt-In Gift"
"Ethical Bribe"
"Irresistible Free Offer" (IFO)

Your Lead Magnet could be a number of different things, depending on your offerings and your Ideal Clients' needs. But in all cases, they are digital. Here are the most commonly used Lead Magnets for a home page:

- A white paper or special report
- A digital or e-Book
- An audio download
- A short training video
- Quizzes or assessments

Now let's have a look as some specific examples of Lead Magnets for different types of businesses.

1. If you are Personal Trainer ...
✓ You could offer a free guide to the best exercises for burning calories.
✓ You could have a "Top Five Foods to Avoid for Lean Muscle" special report.
✓ You could offer a short video or audio with a mindset piece about training and effective exercise.

2. If you are a Chiropractor ...
✓ You could offer a diagram of the most common spinal troubles.
✓ You could have a "Best Posture" booklet that shows ergonomic essentials for sitting, standing and working at a computer.
✓ You could offer an audio recording or video with pain relief visualizations or exercises.

3. If you are a Virtual Assistant ...
✓ You could offer a Special Report on "Entrepreneur's Top Ten Time Wasters."
✓ You could have a small eBook How-To on something most of your Ideal Clients need help with.
✓ You could create an audio or video with organizational tips.

Here are some things you want to keep in mind when it comes to your free gift offer on the website home page:

1. It *must* speak to your Ideal Client's big pain. It must give them some information they are looking for.
2. It should not give them *everything* so that they don't need you!

3.   Keep it short: 10 pages or less; 10 minutes or less. People are busy and they don't have time to dive into a long report or watch a 30-minute video. At least, not at first. Only when you've established some rapport with them and added value, will they likely invest more of their time with you.

4.   Make it automated. Offering a 30-minute call as your initial free gift is a bad idea for most businesses unless you only plan to speak to one or two people per month.

Also, your gift should require a very small commitment on your website visitor's part, so that they can remain almost anonymous. In other words, a "Call for a free consult" is not a good Lead Magnet. You can include that on your website if it's something you offer, but if that's all you offer, you will lose more leads than you will gain and here's why: Most people want to "window shop" a bit before they actually speak with someone. If your website visitor's only option is to call you, but they're not quite ready for that, they'll leave your site and keep looking. And you'll lose what could be a great lead.

At the end of this chapter you'll have the opportunity to brainstorm some great free gifts to offer your website visitors.

The Key to a Great Lead Magnet

The key to a successful Lead Magnet (one that gets the best leads for you) is that it should not be too long, and it should give Ideal Clients some kind of valuable information on the "what" of their problem or the solution they seek. But there's another piece of this as well.

When people land on your website Home Page, they need to find out about that Lead Magnet quickly (remember the WIIFM?). So please keep in mind that you can have the most stellar Lead Magnet in the world, but if your Home Page copy isn't compelling, it will do you no good.

Your Home Page should be singular in focus just below your business banner: it must tell your visitors about your free gift offer, and do it by answering the three-second, three questions, because…

"A Confused Mind Doesn't Buy"

Earlier on I mentioned the "fire hose" affect — when people try to stuff all the most pertinent information on their website Home Page, as if it were a yellow pages ad. The problem with this is two-fold. First of all, since most of us are dealing with information overwhelm on a daily basis, bombarding your site visitors with even more of it will only serve to drive them away. Second, by trying to give new visitors a variety of information all at once, you will more likely create confusion in their minds.

There's an old saying in sales that warns: "A confused mind never buys." And while your website Home Page should *not* be selling anything (unless your site is specifically a storefront), you *do* want your visitors to take a specific action when they are there.

A specific *Call to Action* (referred to in marketing as a CTA), on your website Home Page is essential. Otherwise, your site visitors may skim around a bit and then leave. When that happens, you lose the opportunity to really connect with them on a long-term basis. Instead, what you want is to bring them into your community by collecting their email address.

Opt-In! — What to Include on your Home Page

If you haven't guessed it by now, the Home Page Call to Action (CTA) I'm referring to is this: *"Just put your first name and email address right here to get your complimentary gift."*

That's right, a Home Page is really best used for one thing: to capture qualified leads and prospects — people who want what you've got!

And this means that your Home Page should focus primarily on the benefits of your free gift as it pertains to the specific struggle, obstacle or solution sought by the person visiting your site.

Now What?

Let's recap. We've talked about your website essentials:

1. Your Home Page, which introduces you or your business, fosters trust, initiates some "Know-Like -Trust" rapport, and may include a video or audio recording
2. Your Lead Magnet (free gift offer) that speaks to your site visitor's pain and helps them understand more about the WHAT of their problem. The gift may also give them a tip or two on what to do about their problem or pain or goal.
3. A strong Call to Action, inviting them to exchange their contact information for a copy of the gift.

Now what? Once you've got a list, what do you do next? You engage your potential clients with more rapport-building through email marketing. This is sometimes called a "funnel" or "drip" or "auto sequence" in marketing.

The Lead Magnet Bundle

Together, your Free Gift, Home Page, and Email Funnel comprise what I call your "Lead Magnet Bundle." and they are the first and most important element of your online marketing strategy. You can imagine the Lead Magnet Bundle as a kind of extra-large, virtual catcher's mitt. When you've got a good mitt, you can catch the ball, no matter what angle it comes from!

Your Lead Magnet Bundle needs to be in place first. Before you start focusing on advertising, guest speaking on tele-summits, using Facebook or Twitter to build a following, or anything else that specifically markets your business online. Why? Because as I wrote earlier: You List is Gold. Without it, you can't market to warm prospects. There's really no point in building an online presence until you can capture those leads with your big, virtual catcher's mitt!

There are 2 exceptions to this rule. The first is when your business serves a corporate clientele and your website functions mostly as a place for prospective corporate clients (with corporate budgets) to vet you. The other is if your website is a storefront (think Amazon or Zappos, as examples).

Anatomy of a Beginner Funnel

Let's look at a basic* follow-up sequence, once your website visitor has opted-in to your list.

1. Start with a series of 8-9 emails delivered automatically over the course of about 21 days.
2. Begin the emails with ways to encourage your new list member to use their free gift. It's a way to nurture engagement and add value to their experience with you. It builds trust.

3. Add more value by following up with emails such as: Frequently Asked Questions (answered, of course), a heads up about a particularly popular blog post you've written, or some insider tips.

4. Near the end of the first 21 days, make an offer of some kind. Maybe it's an invitation to a complimentary strategy session or an automated webinar which gives them a choice of when to attend. It could be a special offer on a product or service. Whatever it is, make sure it focuses on this invitation.

5. Follow-up the invitation with a second, "soft reminder" and a deadline for the special price or opportunity.

6. Begin sending weekly or monthly newsletters (called broadcast emails) to everyone after they sign up.

7. Make sure your newsletter includes partial articles that send people back to your blog site once a month, along with periodic offers and specials of your products and service.

8. Send periodic solo emails with offers, invitations to free training events, or the products and services of others which may compliment your own.

*In addition to this basic structure, you can include a low price point ($10 or under) offer immediately after they sign-up. I call this a "welcome offer" but in internet marketing it is sometimes referred to as an "entry offer" or less kindly, a "tripwire." Handle your welcome offer with great care so it is effective. Consult an internet marketing pro to develop the right offer for your business.

Other Must-Haves for Your Website

Below is a list of other pages you want to be sure to have on your website for optimal marketing. Beneath the list you'll find a more detailed description of each.

1. An "About" page. The second most visited website page after the Home Page.
2. A Testimonials page. Let others sing your praise!
3. A Sales Page. These are used for a single, specific product or program you are selling.
4. A Store page. This is great when you have several products or services for sale.
5. A Blog. Smart marketers use blogging as a key component for great website rankings and prospect engagement.
6. The Legal Stuff. Essential for business websites. Be sure to include at least the following:
    a. Privacy Policy
    b. General Disclaimer with Terms and Liability Policy
    c. Contact Information
    d. Refund Policy

You may need or want other pages as well, but these are the minimum requirements. Now, let's have a look at each of these pages in turn.

Your About Page

The About Page of most websites is the most visited page after the Home Page. On the Home Page, you talk about *Them* (your site visitors); on the About Page you get to talk more about you. This is where people get to check you out, grasp something about your message, mission, point of view, and credentials. It is essential that your website has a well-written About Page.

Be sure to avoid a painfully boring, drawn-out CV, with a history of all your jobs, degrees and letters. Snooze-o-rama! Nobody cares about your credentials enough to read an in-depth resume unless you're applying for tenure at an Ivy League university.

Exaggeration aside, your About Page, (even though it's about you), needs to be interesting and engaging to *them*. Provide only the information that tells your readers why you are the one to help them. Sure, you can add in a few friendly facts to illustrate your personality and character — things that differentiate you from others in your marketplace — but remember, they are looking to see if you are the one who can help them. Always write with this in mind!

Your specific credentials can then be included in a brief summary below the compelling/engaging information. You also want to be sure to avoid the big online "No-No's" like huge blocks of text or no sub-headings. Paragraphs should remain short, with a compelling sub-headings placed every two to four paragraphs.

Testimonial Formula

Here is a great formula for testimonials:

"Hi, My Name is _____.
Before I started working with [insert your name or company name] I was [insert problem they were having which you solved]. Now, I'm [insert solution or new circumstance or how they benefited]. Thank you [insert your name or company name]!"

Your Testimonials Page

Social proof is one of the most effective methods for marketing your business. Once someone gets serious about investing in you, they are more than likely going to check out reviews. Make it easy for them, and let others sing your praise!

Consider Trip Advisor. It's no longer possible for crappy hotels or resorts to fake it with pretty pictures. People turn to the experience of others to know who is *legit* ... and who isn't.

The same is true with your website. You want to be sure to have a number of testimonials on your website so your visitors can read first-hand what it's like to work with you or use your business's products or services.

The ideal testimonial is a video, where someone shares their name and then a few of the benefits they experienced from working with you. Videos should be about one minute or less. It's best to provide the person's full name if possible beneath or beside the video. Even better, pull quotes from the testimonial and place them to the side of the video as well, this way your visitor can scan the quotes and select the videos they want to watch.

Second to video is a written testimonial of one or two short paragraphs, a picture and a full name. Again, the same principles apply: They should share something about the benefits they experienced from working with you.

Finally, a written testimonial without picture is possible, but certainly not ideal. Still, it's better than nothing, so if that's all you can get, go ahead and use it until you can begin to accumulate video testimonial or pictures with testimonials.

Sales Pages

Sales Pages don't always stay "live" on a website, but sometimes they do. Sales Pages are generally used for an event-based launch of a new program, product, or service. They're ideal when you want to send a lot of people to your site to sell them into a program or purchase a product or service.

It's not within the scope of this book to cover what's required for a sales page to actually make sales. Suffice to say that copywriters can command thousands, and sometimes tens of thousands of dollars, for a single Sales Page. If and when you are ready to launch a product or program, please, do not try to write one without at least reading up on it a bit. Better yet, hire a good copywriter!

In the meantime, if you would like to learn the fundamental ingredients for the "Anatomy of a Sales Page," and plenty of other copywriting tips, you can access my digital training program, *Website Writing Bootcamp* at http://dawndelvecchio.com/writing-bootcamp/.

I've devoted an entire section of the program to this very subject. It will provide you with a template from which you can begin to build a good Sales Page. (And the rest of the program includes information for your website structure and content too.)

A Store Page

Your Store Page is optional as well. It is best to have one only if you have several products, books or programs to offer.

Don't expect many sales from your Store Page. In time, with enough website visitors, you'll get some, but for the most part, unless your website is a store, your Store Page function is to give visitors a sense of your expertise and areas of specialty. In other words, it adds credential and boosts your position as an expert.

Your Blog

Why is a blog essential? A blog is essential because it makes search engine crawlers happy. As I mentioned earlier, the key ingredients for improving your chances of being found online are relevance and value. The more relevant pages tend to cast a wider net and improve your chances of ranking higher in search results. (More on this below, under the Online Marketing #2.)

This is where fresh content (blog posts) comes in. Adding fresh content to your site on a consistent basis, and then having a strategy for sending visitors to read that content, demonstrates (in an algorithmic kind of way), that your website offers relevant, valuable information.

Here's a formula to explain this concept:

Relevance + Value + Freshness + Sharing = More Website Visitors

1. A consistent blogging schedule can go a long way toward bringing *new* visitors to your website. The formula is simple: Write a relevant blog post.
2. Share the beginning of it on Social Media and in your email newsletters.
3. Put a link for people to continue reading.
4. Get visitors to your website to finish reading!

As a content provider and manager for a number of blog sites over the years, I've used this strategy for list-building and search engine ranking, and I can tell you, it works! The trick is to be consistent (once a week is good, three- to five a week is better, once a month is minimum) be relevant, make sure each post is SEO optimized (see below for more on SEO), and share the heck out of it across the web.

The Legal Stuff

Finally, there are some pages you must have no matter what your business, service or products. These include the following:

1. A Contact Page. Search engine algorithms give more weight to sites that provide visitors with a way to contact you. (And besides, it's good business). You'll have a hard time being ranked on search engines, no matter how great your website is, if you don't have a Contact Page with a real way for people to email or call you. This is about transparency and it's a no-brainer really, for conscientious business owners.

2. Privacy Policy. This is required if you are going to collect names and email addresses. You want to promise you won't sell their contact information. Again, this is about transparency and trust-building with your website visitors.

3. Refund Policy. Obviously this only applies if you are selling products and services through your website.

4. Disclaimer. This is your general Terms and Conditions Page. Check out your industry leaders' websites for ideas on this, then consult your attorney for a proper Disclaimer Page for you.

Please be sure to consult your attorney for the correct terms and conditions to include for the Legal Stuff, based on your business, offerings and the laws of your State or Country.

Beyond Your Website

Now that we've looked closely at the core elements of a good website for marketing success, let's look at some of the other things you want to consider when marketing your business online.

Online Marketing #2: SEO

You know the acronym SEO. You may wonder what it means. You hear conflicting reports and think, "Oh brother, I think I'm getting a headache!" SEO stands for Search Engine Optimization, and for people (like me and maybe you) who find acronyms annoying at best and revolting at worst, the word alone can be off-putting. So I'm going to give you a short, sweet run-down of what you need to know about SEO.

Let's start with you. Imagine you are looking for Kitty Pajamas for your niece who is five years old and only wears the color yellow these days. What are you going to do? Are you going to go to every clothing store in town to see if they happen to have yellow kitty pajamas for five year olds? Probably not.

Are you going to look up a very broad category like "pajamas" online? Or, are you going to look up "yellow kitty pajamas for girls" so that you don't get results for boys pajamas, adult pajamas, pajamas with puppies, fish, elephants, Teenage Mutant Ninja Turtles ... or pajamas that aren't yellow.

Now let's say you click the link that comes up at the top of the "organic" search results (not the ads at the very top or the side, but the regular results, called "organic"), but all you find is a store that sells plastic, pink, Hello Kitty toys. What are you going to do?

You're going to go back to that search results page and try the next result on the page. And so it goes until you find what you want.

Now think about how long it might take you to find your niece's dream pajamas if all you did was search "pajamas." (Hint: You're better off going to the kids clothing section of every single store in your county or State!) But as you get more specific, your chances of finding what you are looking for (relevant and valuable) increase dramatically.

99

Google, Relevance, and Organic?

The folks at Google, the most widely used search engine on the planet, want you to find what you want — quickly and easily. After all, the easier it is for you to find what you want, the more likely you are to trust and return to Google as your preferred search engine. In other words, they want your business. That's why their advanced algorithms keep poorly optimized websites low on the organic rankings. It's also why Google leads the way for other search engines to follow suit.

The reason you can be super specific and find relevant information for your imaginary niece's gift is because of the power and sophistication of search engines, *plus* the websites that have smartly optimized for "yellow kitty pajamas for girls." So then, SEO begins with optimizing your site to be search-engine-friendly to the specific keywords and phrases you want for the highest possible ranking.

Longevity Builds Trust

Another natural and very organic way to improve your rankings over time (besides relevance and freshness and geeky stuff like SEO) is longevity. Simply by being on the web for some time (and having frequent visitors who don't leave your site as soon as they get there) will give your website a longevity advantage.

How Do You Do SEO?

Optimizing your website for SEO begins with keyword research related to the following:

1. Your particular offerings.

2. How people search for those offerings (what keywords and phrases they type in when they search).

3. Competition for those keywords and phrases (how many others in your industry are using a keyword or phrase).

Once you determine the optimal keywords for your website, you will use them in very specific places on your website and within your blog posts. The most important of these places is your Home Page. Other keywords can be used to optimize specific pages and blog posts.

Other ways to optimize your site include:

1. Use compelling, engaging writing that speaks to the concerns of your visitors in the language they naturally use, so that your visitors stay on your site longer.

2. Add lots of *value* in the form of easily understood, user-friendly information.

3. Make sure every page of your site is reader friendly by avoiding excess information, huge blocks of unbroken text and other, reader-unfriendly content or images.

4. Fix all broken links.

5. Make sure your link structure is sound.

6. Include internal linking (linking one article or page to another within your website) *when it's relevant.*

7. Avoid loading your site with outbound links (links that send people away from your website).

8. Use title tags and meta descriptions.

The above information is very basic. My intention here is simply to give you a general *concept* of what's involved with SEO. There are plenty of SEO pros out there who can optimize your site in a comprehensive way. So if you are keen to get high rankings fast, it's worth consulting a specialist.

But remember: without a solid Lead Magnet Bundle (your giant catcher's mitt) in place first, investing in a professional to optimize your site is putting the cart before the horse!

Online Marketing #3: Social Media

There's definitely some confusion about using social media for business. Social media gets bandied about in some circles as if it is the magic bullet for getting more customers, making more money, and generally improving your business bottom line. I'm here to tell you the truth ... it's not.

Social media in and of itself is not a business strategy. It's not a marketing strategy all by itself either. And it's certainly not worth a considerable amount of your precious time (or money!) until you have other business essentials in place. Essentials like ...

- Solid Sales Skills
- A Marketing Plan that includes both online and offline elements.
- A way to network and promote your business in LIVE situations (you know: meeting people!)
- An optimized website (remember the giant catcher's mitt?)
- A Social Media Marketing *Plan.*

That's my caveat. Now, with these points in mind, let's have a look at Marketing Strategies for the "Biggies" in the Social Media arena.

Marketing Strategies for Facebook

Facebook can make you money, but you have to set up a marketing strategy the right way. And again, without the above essentials, you can expect limited results.

The first thing you want to do is set up a Fan Page and start to build your fan base. In time, you can also advertise. But the most important thing to keep in mind with Facebook is that people are not there to shop. They're not there to buy stuff and they don't like leaving Facebook.

The folks at Facebook have thought about this of course, and have implemented some tools like Facebook Landing Pages and Facebook advertising in order to bridge the gap between pure marketing and a "social by nature" type of platform. But in the end, it is still a connection-building place more than a sales platform. So use it the way it was meant to be used: to be social, build rapport, and create trust.

Also keep in mind that Facebook changes all the time. In the early days when I was building a fan base for a page I managed, I got the page's "likes" up into the multiple thousands, single-handedly and without spending a red cent — in under three months! These were the glory days before Facebook advertising. Now it's a lot harder to get that kind of reach, and you need multiple strategies in order to build fan momentum. Add to this the fact that Facebook is changing all the time, and you've got a formula for uncertainty at best.

There are many great marketing pros out there who specialize in Facebook. They keep their finger on the pulse of this ever-changing leviathan. So when you have all your good website stuff in place, you can consult an expert or take a workshop or hire a social media pro to handle this aspect of your business for you.

Other Social Media: Twitter, Linked In, Google+ and the (*Pinte*)Rest!

LinkedIn

If you serve other businesses (B2B) or simply want to ensure a professional presence online, LinkedIn is an essential. Unlike Facebook, LinkedIn is about making professional connections. It functions differently than Facebook, but shares a common theme: engagement.

Having a profile and making connections on LinkedIn is good, but joining key groups and participating in discussions is better.

To Tweet or Not to Tweet

"Larry" (The name of the Twitter bird), may be a familiar friend to you. I like him just fine, but don't deal much with him. Twitter is all about engagement in sound bites of no more than 140 characters (including spaces!) Twitter is where #hashtags came from and the platform can be a real business builder when you make the effort.

As with the rest of the Social Media platforms, the best way to get started with Twitter is to, well, *start*. Once you can make your way around, if you like it, then find an expert, training class, or assistant who can work ole Larry for your business leads.

G+

Google Plus was created by Google (so the rumors say) in an effort to compete with Facebook. When it was first launched in September of 2011, people proclaimed it would make Facebook obsolete.

Obviously, no such thing has happened, but Google+ is still a viable place to create authority in your field. This is because when you create a G+ profile and then link it with other content of yours on the web (your website, YouTube and elsewhere) it serves as an "authorship tool" which will connect that content directly to you. This is why you will find some Google search results have the name, picture and profile information of the person who created the content.

You can think of G+ as a kind of social proof "layer" for your business credentials. By the way, G+ is the second most used Social Media site on the web. (Facebook being first, of course), and has 540 million monthly active users according to Wikipedia.

Pinterest and Instagram

Pinterest and Instagram have gained plenty of popularity due to their undeniable visual appeal. If your business sells products, use these platforms to creatively position them. If your business is service-based then your images can be a combination of theme-based images and pictures of you doing whatever it is you do (speaking, coaching, teaching, etc.)

Again, as with all of the social media platforms, try it out, get the basics down, and if you find it will serve you, get the proper training or hire someone with experience to manage your business presence on these platforms.

Online Marketing #4: Beyond Social Media — Expert Positioning Online

There are other ways to increase your visibility and build your credibility online. The first of these is expert positioning through other people's platforms. Becoming a guest speaker on a few tele-summits or a guest blogger on popular blog sites (sites that get a lot of visitors and engagement) are great ways to position yourself as an expert. This will also help you get more visitors stopping by your website.

One of the best ways to find these opportunities is to make connections with other experts in your field or complementary industries. As an example, let's say you specialize in EFT (Emotional Freedom Technique). You may find experts in all kinds of arenas where EFT could apply. Some of the leaders in this field (or the internet savvy ones, anyway) may host live chats, tele-summits, or blog sites. You could reach out to them to find out what it would take to be a guest speaker or guest blogger for them.

Here's another example. Maybe you are a Nutrition Coach. Why not see if there are any tele-summits specializing in weight loss or mindset, nutrition, GMOs, or even things like prenatal care?

YouTube

Traditionally, (as if there is much tradition when it comes to the online world), YouTube could be considered a part of "social media," and in a sense, it really is. But I have given it a space of its own here because of its power as a marketing tool.

YouTube is owned by Google. It also ranks as #2 for search engines. That's right, even though this is a video platform, it serves, willy nilly, as a search engine too.

This piece of information alone should turn on a light bulb in your head ... V I D E O. If you aren't using it, it's time. In fact, to *not* use video as a part of your online marketing strategy is foolhardy. You may recall, I suggested that video is a necessity on your Home Page.

Video can be used in many ways, from *"vlogs"* (video blog posts) to straight social media marketing (building a YouTube following). Video also serves the powerful purpose of establishing Brand Trust. After all, it's one thing to read about a business, it's another to watch and listen to the owner of that business speak authentically about topics that have meaning to them! (Remember the Know-Like-Trust Factor.)

Video, in today's virtual market place, is the fastest and most effective way to create authority and trust, and the very best way to do it is by being authentic and in integrity. How's that for great news?

Video Strategy for Small Budgets

When you think about marketing as a whole, you want to keep in mind that the biggest fish in the industry are TV advertisers. Almost anywhere in the world, the best ads with the biggest budgets will be TV ads. What this means to you, the small business owner, is that your market is used to that kind of advertising, and they're used to it at a high level of quality and sophistication.

Now before you get nervous thinking you have to go out and purchase a video studio and animation team, let me tell you that you don't need that! What you do need though, is YOU. You on video talking to your Ideal Clients and customers.

Let's face it, even though YouTube is the second most used search engine in the world, it's *not* full of high-tech, high-budget videos. Most are homemade, do-it-yourself varieties with no special effects and not much in the way of good lighting. Nonetheless, some very low-tech videos are garnering thousands of views thanks to their novelty, relevance, trust-worthiness, and marketing savvy.

If you haven't tried making videos for your online marketing campaigns, I strongly urge you to consider it. The more you can build a presence on YouTube, the better chances you have of increasing your Google rankings and building loyal fans and followers.

Online Marketing #5: Advertising

Online advertising can skyrocket your business when you have awesome ads, a targeted audience and something compelling to sell. As with all of the other online marketing recommendations I've made, your ad dollars will only work if you've got that big fat catcher's mitt and/or a stellar Sales Page for whatever you are advertising.

You can use ads on many search engines, not just Google. And of course, you can also use them on Facebook. Banner advertising on different websites can also serve you, depending on your business and on which sites you choose to place your ads.

The nice thing about advertising online is that you can experiment while keeping your investment low. This is because you can set your budget in advance. Another nice thing about online advertising is how specifically you can target your audience.

To illustrate this last point, here are some examples of the kind of specificity I'm talking about on both Facebook and Google:

Facebook

In Facebook, you can specify who your ads will reach in all kinds of ways, including:

- Demographic (like age range, location, gender, languages spoken)
- Interests
- Type of work
- Ethnic affinity
- Political leanings
- Relationship status
- Education level
- Purchasing behaviors
- Types of devices they use
- Hobbies ... among others!

Google

You can't get quite as specific with Google because, unlike Facebook, people don't share their private leanings, their connections, or their interests on Google. Still, you can narrow the audience who will see your ads based on some very specific criterion, like:

- Where they live
- Languages they speak, and most importantly ...
- Keywords they use to search for things

The down side of online advertising is that, like everything else online, things change and improve quickly — including the best ways to advertise effectively. That's why, when you are ready to invest in an online ad campaign, it is well worth your time to investigate what's currently working and what's not. The best way to start is by educating yourself on the basics, and then outsourcing to a professional.

If hiring someone to create your online ad campaigns is not an option for your budget just yet, you can do the following. Research to gather some free information on the different types of advertising, then read a book or two on advertising for the platform where you'd like to place your ads. After that, give it a try! Be sure to use the split testing method too (testing two different ads with only one change for two to three days, then eliminating the lower performing ad).

As you start to get some traction with your ads, and if you have some budget, go ahead and hire a consultant to take you to the next level.

You Are Awesome!

Phew! That was a lot of cut-n-dry, eh?

It's why I want to take a moment right now to turn the spotlight back on you, my dear Holistic Business Owner ...

Remember, no matter how techy, dry, or well, *boring* all of this marketing business may be, there's a priceless reason behind it: YOU. Whatever your gifts, skills and calling, you have been guided in a Sacred way to this seemingly not-so-sacred strategy stuff. So please, give yourself a high-five, a hug, an organic cookie ... you are awesome!

And you are here for a reason. Your Soul Purpose Calling is needed because it can serve many. What you do solves problems and makes a real difference in people's lives — as long as they can find you.

So to reiterate what I wrote at the beginning of Part II, in order for your high calling to take hold, you need that reach (through marketing strategies). This is what allows you to bring in the capital required to keep your business — and you! — afloat.

You really *can* do this. You really can reach a bigger audience, make a bigger difference and *thrive*. Sure, it's a step-by-step process. And yes, it's always better to invest in support and mentorship (like you're doing by reading this book!). So keep going.

Even if this doesn't all make sense to you right now, it's okay. With time and a commitment to doing your good work in the world, even the most challenging aspects of running a business eventually get easier.

Tying it All Together

Now, when it comes to marketing your business, there is a great deal to consider. Good marketing and outreach requires you to plan strategically, then invest money wisely and consistently in your outreach and promotional campaigns. This means you'll sometimes have to make tough decisions. Decisions about your time. Decisions about your money.

Thanks to the internet, you have the opportunity to reach a lot more people and, when done well, make a lot more money. But it also means that you've got to learn more and invest more in this powerful marketing medium.

In fact, with the advent of the internet and search engines, getting the word out about your business **to the people who are looking for your help** has never been easier. Instead of trying to broadcast news about your business to everyone in your city (or everyone who shares your Yellow Pages), you can use the world wide web to put yourself directly in the path of someone who wants what you've got to offer.

In Part II we looked at a number of strategies for proper, affordable (often free), and ethical marketing for you and your valuable services. The problem is, no matter how many great marketing opportunities are out there today, without the right relationship to money, no marketing plan will be effective. That's why **Part III is all about your relationship to Money.**

Faulty beliefs about money, service, and success are the root cause of many small business failures — particularly among those who share in common the values of the Holistic Business Owner.

In Part III we're going to dive deep into this emotionally-charged and oft-confusing topic: How we think about money; how we react to money; how Toxic Conversations (most within our own heads) keep us without money; how to reframe the way we talk and think about money; and ultimately, how to heal our relationship with money.

But before we do that, and in order to tie together the key take-aways for this section, be sure to give yourself some time to go through the exercises below. This will help you summarize what we've covered in Part II. It will also help you gain clarity about which online and offline marketing strategies would best serve your business at this time.

EXERCISE 1: Your Ideal Lead Magnet

In order to make the most of your website (and create that "giant catcher's mitt"), you need a way to collect the leads of those people who visit your site and show interest in your products or services.

As you consider what kind of gift you want to offer your website visitors, be sure it meets the following criterion:

1. It is digital, so there is no cost for delivery.
2. It is brief, so your prospects are more likely to read, watch or listen to it.
3. It is automated, so you don't have to do anything in order for a prospect to receive it.
4. It answers the question "What?" that your prospects are asking.
5. It adds value to your prospect and positions you as an authority.

With these things in mind, sketch out your ideal lead magnet below.

EXERCISE 2: Three Questions in Three Seconds

Since your website Home Page is the first stop for most of your visitors, you want to be sure to convey the key information they need in order to grab their attention and inform them about your complimentary gift. And with just three seconds, this means you want to be **Clear, Concise**, and of course, *Compelling*.

With this in mind, take some time now to write out the answers to the three most important questions people are silently asking themselves when they land on your website. You may also refer to the exercises you completed in Part I when you first started thinking about these questions and your Ideal Client.

1. What is it? (What is this website about?)

_____

_____

2. Who is it for?

_____

_____

3. What's in it for me (WIIFM)?

_____

_____

EXERCISE 3: Mapping the Marketing Plan

In Part II we looked at six different offline marketing strategies (Networking, Advertising, Snail Mail, The "100 lb." Phone, Sponsorships, and Speaking) and five different online marketing strategies (Your Website, SEO, Social Media, Expert Positioning Online and Advertising). Now is your chance to consider all of these possible ways to reach your audience and get the word out about your business.

The exercise below will help you see all of these possibilities and begin to map out a sane and scalable marketing plan moving forward.

1.   A few things to keep in mind: Choose what is possible for you without overwhelm! You can always add on additional strategies later.

2.   Make sure to include offline strategies. It's much easier to build that all important, "know-like-trust" factor when people can actually meet you. Plus, you will be better able to invest in your online marketing when you are making money through your contacts made through low-cost, "old fashioned" strategies like networking, speaking and the 100lb. phone.

Your Outreach Plan

Have a look at all of the possible ways you can market your business presented in the chart below. Give some thought to each of these and then make notes in the space provided about how you might use each of these strategies in your business.

Once you've given each strategy some consideration, go back over them all and circle only those that seem feasible for you at this time. Choose ones that you can afford the time, energy, and money in which to invest. Be sure to circle some in the offline column and some in the online column.

When you've narrowed your selection based on feasibility for you right now, look at each one in turn and ask the following question: "Is this a 'low hanging fruit' strategy in which I can turn my efforts into income quickly ... or is it a long-term strategy?" In other words, will this strategy deliver results in days or weeks, or something that will deliver over time?

Put a star next to those that will provide you with quick results.

Now you should have a very clear idea of what's possible for you. You want to act on your starred items right away and begin implementing at least one circled item from each column.

Jot down at least one way to use each of these strategies.

Offline Strategy	Online Strategy
Networking	Website
Advertising	SEO
"Snail Mail"	Social Media
Booths & Sponsorships	Expert Positioning
The 100 lb. Phone	Advertising
Speaking	

For People Ready to Eliminate Financial Blocks to Business Success ...

RE:Visioning Your Inner Blueprint

A Special Gift from Dawn
RE:Visioning

"A Simple Way to RE*view* and RE*vise* your Inner "Vision" of Money, Service & Success, so you can Eliminate Financial Struggle, Make a Bigger Difference with your Gifts, and Grow a Business that Lets you *THRIVE!*"

RE:Visioning is a powerful method for eliminating harmful programming of any kind – at a subconscious level. The process is easy to do and ideal for the heart-centered visionary who longs to bring their gifts to the world in a bigger way, but struggles with financial limitation.

http://www.SpiritMindMoneyBook.com/re-vision

You can use the **RE:Visioning** process to ...

✓ Eliminate negative, subconscious programming about money .
✓ Effectively *do* what you came here to do, and thrive in the process.
✓ Swiftly transform your inner conversation around money so that it serves the highest GOOD of all.
✓ Set up a new *operating system* around abundance.
✓ Take effective, integrated action to earn the money you need.
✓ Transform your relationship to Money, Service and Success!

Grab Your Own Inner Blueprint for Success with a Complimentary Copy of the **RE:Visioning** Process

Access your copy and start your RE:Visioning right away, simply go to:

http://www.SpiritMindMoneyBook.com/re-vision

PART III: MONEY

If you've been lighting candles, setting affirmations, invoking abundance, trying every manifestation technique in the book, or simply been 'playing and praying' to win the lottery ... but you still don't have a thriving business, you *need* to read this section!

Part III is all about your relationship to *Money* and how that impacts your business. For many readers, this will be the linchpin for you — the key piece of our conversation around *Service* and *Success* that can springboard you to a new and better place.

In Part III we're going to dive deep into the emotionally-charged and oft-confusing topic of cash — How we think about it, how we react to it and how, what I am referring to here as a "toxic" blueprint about money, is a guarantee that we'll never have enough of it.

We're going to look at some of the ways you may be structuring your thinking about money that actually undermines your dreams and goals — for your business and your life.

It's okay to feel uncomfortable here. And it's okay if you feel like it will take some time to handle this. Whatever arises for you during this part of the book is a-okay. I'm going to stay with you. Just please, please, stay with me.

You see, in order to deal with chronic financial struggle, and assuage the pain it invariably creates, many of us turn to coping mechanisms (including behaviors, thought patterns, and spiritual explanations) that don't actually work. Now, these may have served us initially, but ultimately, they'll never give us the freedom to make positive changes in our income. And if you are or want to be a business owner, this can spell disaster.

I'll argue (hopefully convincingly), that these coping mechanisms, internal talk tracks, and unexamined money "mantras" we use to avoid or minimize the issue, actually serve to *undermine* us and our financial wellbeing.

My Promise

I will do my best not to come off sounding judgmental or critical, and ... I *will* be direct. My goal here is to share with you some key lessons that I had to learn the hard way. I do this in hopes that fewer people will have to struggle for as long as I did, before they can really *serve* and *thrive*.

I recognize that when we are in a lot of pain about something, it's very easy to shut down, dismiss, or reject the information being delivered. So I want to request again that you stay with me here. I struggled for years with the mindset pieces, unexamined money mantras, and plain old *confusion* about Money's pivotal role in relation to Service and Success that you'll find in this part of the book. If what I went through can help you avoid or reduce struggle, it will have been worth it.

Chapter Six
Toxic Money Blueprint

A Losing Proposition ...

In order to run a successful business, however small or large, it's essential that we have an internal blueprint which aligns with success. When we have confusion and pain around money, we cannot create a success-focused business. Instead, the negative conversations and/or unexamined beliefs we have will undermine us. They'll undermine our hard work, our heartfelt commitment, our vision and yep, our bank accounts. This is what I am calling a "toxic" blueprint about money, and when you've got one, it's not possible to grow a successful business, serve others effectively, or thrive personally.

ഇാര

You were meant to thrive. And if the Universe/God/Divine had the wherewithal to seed a dream within you, it most certainly has the abundance to provide you with it.

ഇാര

The subconscious beliefs and subsequent actions associated with a Toxic Blueprint invariably lead to negative and even harmful results. These results are negative for the business owner, who may struggle, endure cycles of burn-out, or eventually fail. But they're also negative for the people who could benefit from products and services which that failed business (or burnt-out owner) could have provided.

It's a lose-lose proposition for all involved. That's why, in this part of the book we will focus specifically on the money mindsets, unexamined money mantras (the conversations), and behaviors that make up this template for trouble. Then we'll have a look at the habits of mind and behavior needed in order to "detoxify" from outworn notions about money, so that you can **do what you love, make a difference,** and *thrive.*

Experience Not Theory

I write this from experience, not theory. So please, even if this topic is making you uncomfortable, I urge you yet again, to stay with me. Your skills, services, and vision ARE needed. If Spirit/God/Divine had the wherewithal to seed a vision and purpose within you, then the same force of All That Is *absolutely* has the wherewithal to provide a thriving living for you.

But there's a caveat to that universal promise: It is you who will have to cooperate with the vision. You will have to clear up any contrary (often subconscious) beliefs, habits, and unexamined ideas that can block your success. And you will have to take the actions needed to create a thriving business. When you use what is offered here to gain insight, you are taking the first step toward healing and wholing your relationship to **Money, Service, and Success.**

After all, awareness of a problem is the first step in solving it.

As with the other two sections, I'll provide you with some exercises at the end of Part III. Obviously though, unlike the previous two parts, the exercises in this section are more soul-searching in nature.

Uncomfortable? Perhaps. A potential gold mine for your business success? Absolutely! So then, let's dive in!

Money, Service, and Success

There's a lot of confusion about the intersection of money, service, and success. It runs the gamut from avoiding evil by staying broke, (wanting money means you're greedy; money is, or will make you immoral; too much of it and it becomes filthy lucre; it's the root of all evil ...) to an attitude that borders on spiritual smugness.

I know that sounds harsh, so please hear me out. When we take a faith-based approach to the pragmatic reality of business building, all kinds of weird notions can undermine our efforts. These are false beliefs about the nature of our material reality and they don't work as a business plan.

Here are some examples of these misguided notions:

> *"The universe will provide because I'm a good person helping others."*
> *"My work is highly sacred, so I can't charge a set amount for it."*
> *"If it's meant to be, it will be."*
> *"My good/bad karma is why this is/isn't working out."*

More on this in a moment.

The False Beliefs of a *Spiritually Justified* Poverty Mindset

I want to point out that, for many holistically-focused business owners, there's a gap between service and money. This gap unfolds as a false belief system which, when examined logically, doesn't actually make much sense.

This false belief system equates:

- Struggle with Goodness
- Poverty with Decency
- Limited Means with Spiritual Cleanliness
- Chronic Financial Burden with Integrity

Folks ... this has got to stop. We are all going to HAVE to dig into our assumptions — our sacred cow beliefs — and clear out these antiquated ideas obstructing our life's operating system. These old beliefs about money, service, and success have no business being in your business at the cusp of the Age of Aquarius.

It's time to heal and transform them.

When we choose not to examine old-paradigm attitudes we may be carrying in our subconscious minds about money, the avoidance itself will keep us locked-in to money troubles. In business this is absolute. But even as an employee, toxic ideas about money will keep you down. The difference is this: An employee can manage their lives based on clearly defined income, *without* needing to spend money on growing a business. A business owner on the other hand, has no such luxury.

That's why if you want to run a *business* it is crucial to look at the beliefs you hold about money squarely in the face. When you don't, they lead rapidly to ineffectual business behaviors like chronic inefficiency; an unwillingness to take actionable steps to improve yourself or your business; excessive vacillation over decisions; fear of investing in business growth; and sadly — a resistance (often subconscious) to learning even basic business skills.

When we don't treat our business like a business because we're locked into fear or false beliefs about money, it results in poor judgments, ineffectual actions, and limited success at best. At worst, burnout and resentment ensue, followed by a dejected return to a job or even a health crisis "wake-up" call.

As long as your mindset around **Money, Service, and Success** is wounded by outdated, pseudo-religious notions of meek camels, tainted money-lenders or "worldly defilements," you will never really BE or DO and you certainly won't ever HAVE, what you intended when you came here.

Getting Down to Business

Now that I've painted a picture of the problem, let's get down to business, shall we? To begin, let me ask you a quick question: Why are you in business? Go ahead and answer in your mind or write it down: Why are you in business?

I Am in Business to:

_____.

The WHOLE Answer

If your answer did not include "to make money," you've got something to look at here. I know it's easy to say things like "to help," or "to inspire," or "to be of service," or more specific things like "to serve people with my skills as a (teacher, doctor, coach, therapist, etc.)." But the bottom line is that if you are not also in business to make a living, you don't have a *business* — you have a *hobby*.

Business is about providing for a demand (service) in exchange for money. Not simply one or the other. The good news is, it's possible to have a business that makes money and is of high service.

But if you confuse business with service or Soul Purpose, you won't have a business for very long. One of the most unfortunate situations I ever encountered came from a friend who confused these two very different things.

Ed Goes to Istanbul

Through to his very core, Ed is a teacher. As a long-time yogi, meditation instructor, Reiki master, and hypnotherapist, Ed is in service to uplift humanity. He is strong, fit, funny, and spiritually committed.

A couple of years ago, Ed went to Istanbul. Sounds cool, eh? In his case, it wasn't. You see, Ed had made an inner vow to run his business solely on love offerings. Now I don't know how much Ed invested over the years to gain his many certifications, but I have got to guess it was more than a love offering.

Ed struggled. He had two daughters from a former marriage and was expecting his first grandchild. For most of his adult life, Ed fought depression, poverty, and chronic health conditions. Thankfully, his beloved wife worked hard and brought home the proverbial bacon. But in the wake of a failing economy, Ed's wife lost her job.

Suddenly, life changed radically for them, and because Ed's love offering business never permitted him to build a nest egg for emergencies, he had to take drastic action. Ed moved overseas to teach English, leaving behind his wife for a minimum 1-year contract. Ouch!

Unfortunately, the story gets worse. Due to living conditions in this developing country, Ed contracted some kind of infection which triggered a chronic ailment he had managed to keep in-check for years. So not only did he spend many months apart from his spouse, he returned in poor health. In fact, he was classifiably disabled and had to turn to public assistance just for basic needs.

To me, this is an extreme and sad example of what happens when we have a poor business mindset. Please keep in mind, I'm not saying that love offerings in certain contexts are wrong. In fact, when you are trying out a new service or program, offering a workshop or talk to build contacts, or mastering a new modality, love offerings can be ideal. But as a sole business model? Love offerings simply *are not* a business model.

Had Ed made a different choice about his mastery ... that it was worth paying for; that love offerings aren't a sound model for a business; that *investing* in some business skills would be wise ... he may never have found himself in the shoes he now wears.

Today, Ed is beginning to recover. His health is ever so slowly on the mend, but more than that, he has begun to look at his issues around money and service.

Recently, Ed and I spoke. I was able to share with him a pivotal conversation we once had. A conversation which made it clear to me that Ed was on the road to trouble. A conversation that sent me in a very different direction with my own business.

I had been visiting him and his family during a short summer road trip. After dinner one evening we were talking about some of his financial concerns. I asked Ed how he priced his different services. His attitude and his answer stunned me. With a "there's no room for argument here" tone in his voice, Ed stated his unbending position about pricing: "I will not charge a set fee for my work. My business is based on love donations only."

This statement stopped me in my tracks because it didn't make logical sense in the context of our conversation about his already significant money struggles. But more than the surprise of this smart man's logical incongruence, was his rigid attitude about it.

At the time, I just backed down and changed the subject. Clearly there was no room for discussion. But Ed's statement stuck with me as I watched him — over the course of the next two or more years — descend into health and financial troubles that are the stuff of nightmares.

When Ed and I spoke recently, I shared that memory with him, and how it had sent me on a trajectory to heal my wounds and confusion around money. He was able to see how that belief, and the pain he had around valuing his expertise and asking for money, had been a major source of the difficulties he's had since.

Today, Ed is ready to heal that old mindset and make new choices about his work and his money. But it's a steep uphill climb.

Giving From an Empty Vessel

Ed's story is one of many I could share with you. It's called giving from an empty vessel, and the results are predictable — burn-out, misery and quite possibly disease.

He is not alone in his discomfort around the critical role money plays in successfully serving others through the entity of a business. There are far too many of us in the healing, wellness, and service industries who are suffering from a deep disconnect around cash. That's why I believe it's time we look plainly at any remaining myths, outdated beliefs, and downright lies about the connection between Sacred Service and Financial Stability.

We've come to believe the spin about money (or the "love" of it, anyway) being the root of all evil and then comfort ourselves with righteous poverty. This doesn't work. And I'm going to stick my neck out here and say that it is those of us who struggle the most financially who are most likely to compromise our values, at some point, for the sake of survival. More on this in a moment.

The outworn notion that wanting an abundance of money for our efforts is somehow disdainful has no place in a market economy. After all, we live in a world where money is the system of exchange, and the ever-increasing cost of living impacts even the most heart-felt healers among us.

I want to propose to you that one of the biggest reasons why many of us struggle with the money piece is because we don't want to do the one thing *every single business owner MUST do* ... SELL. That's right, when you are in business, you are in the business of sales. If this comes as a shock to you, then please stay with me. Because if you don't work this through, your business will likely fail.

I deeply believe that in order for us to create a more sustainable world, those of us on a spiritual and conscious path must lead the way. And that means, among other things, charging what the valuable, life-transforming services we offer are worth. It means saying "no!" to the income equivalent of crumbs, once and for all. And it means *asking for the sale*.

The Low Price of High Service

Not that long ago I came across a flyer in a health food store. It was someone offering therapeutic massage. His price: $20 an hour. You read that right: $20 dollars an hour.

Now you've got two ways to look at this: You might think, "Twenty bucks for a massage? I'm in! Give me his number!" Or, you might look at this from a different perspective, one grounded in abundance rather than scarcity. From this perspective you may think, "Twenty bucks for an hour? No Way!"

After all, how can any business owner grow (or even survive comfortably!) making $20 an hour in the United States? Unless you live with mom and dad, are independently wealthy or have no expenses, you'd have to give at least 80 massages a month simply to eke out $1600 per month. That's 20 massages per week before all the other activities you'd need to do to build your client base, maintain and market your business.

This begs the question: **Who would want to go to a massage therapist who will inevitably burn out by giving so much for so little?**

But it's exactly this group of people who face a sometimes insurmountable challenge — a toxic belief (often subconscious), that equates sacred service of any kind with antiquated vows of poverty. Those vows silence us when it's time to ask for the sale.

Instead, we default to bargain-basement pricing in order to make the offer so sweet that we don't have to ask. Bad plan. Yet this is the unfortunate strategy for many healers and helpers, and it comes from a faulty equation that **Sacred Service = Vow of Poverty**.

This equation tells us that if we've got a way to help or even heal others, then we've got an obligation to charge so little that anyone can turn to us — even those so broke that they can't pay attention. The false assumption embedded in this belief implies that you are somehow responsible for other people's wellbeing, their financial circumstances, or their decisions about prioritizing how they choose to spend their money.

However, when we think this argument through, we can see how little sense it makes. So if you struggle to charge abundantly for your services (or even charge at all!) then consider this. When you chronically undercharge, you are telling yourself and your clients that "my mastery, my skills, and my expertise shouldn't be valued as much as other services providers, like a mechanic's, a lawyer's, an MD, insurance agent, or computer technician."

Ask yourself this: Is it your responsibility to give away your hard-earned skills at the expense of your own right livelihood? Is it your responsibility or obligation to give from a diminishing (and eventually empty) vessel? Is it your obligation to sacrifice the quality of your life for an outdated notion of goodness? Perhaps most important of all — Is avoiding the pain of asking for what your services are worth, worth the price of the results you're guaranteed by under-charging?

The Irony of the Moral High Ground

The irony of using spiritual justifications to undercharge is that, instead of doing the right thing, we put ourselves at greater risk of compromising our morals under economic duress.

"Self-righteous and broke" is how one friend described it. And while that may seem unkind, it's not untrue. When we are tempted to stand by an argument that says what we do is too high and holy to charge an appropriate fee, we'll soon count ourselves among the Eds of the world. And then what?

Let's be clear. *None of us* are more clean, more pure, more ethical, or any nearer to a distant heaven if we undercharge for our time. Broke is not a badge to earn. It is a result of a gap in thinking and a lack of sales and marketing skills.

In fact, there's an inversely proportional relationship between your earnings and your willingness to compromise your morals. After all, when you can't make ends meet, you are way more likely than the next guy or gal to find yourself strung over the proverbial barrel.

- Lowering your standards in service or quality in products to cut corners or save energy?
- Making excuses to reduce the number of people you serve because you're burnt-out and pissed off and can't take one more complaint?
- Bitching at your kids or spouse because you're having a bad day?
- Lying to creditors?

- Buying cheap stuff created through exploitative means because Fair Trade is too pricey?

These are hardly the qualities found on the moral high-ground. Yet all too often, when we are burnt-out from overwhelm and low income, we fudge.

From Pain to Platitude — The Self-Defeating Spiritual Bypass

When we're faced with the pain of struggle, burn-out, or failure, it's easy to use religious or spiritual justifications for our circumstances. These justifications serve to ease our pain temporarily with a kind of divine balm or band-aid. But ultimately, like a band-aid, such justifications ring hollow, because they don't heal the essential wound.

Worse still, when we resort to justifications or platitudes to explain away our inability to turn a Soul Purpose vision into a materially viable success, it leads to some very sticky, quasi-spiritual explanations. Explanations that undermine us further.

This kind of thinking is called **Spiritual Bypass**, and it's the culprit behind many failed businesses and financially crippled lives. The term Spiritual Bypass was first used by John Welwood in 1984. Welwood is an author and Clinical Psychologist who noticed a tendency in his clients and himself to use spiritual teachings in order to avoid painful feelings.

The results can include a Pollyanna denial of problems, or even an attitude about our goodness and our struggle that borders on self-righteous. This blocks our ability to own what's really going on, and *prevents* us from taking the steps necessary for effective change.

While Spiritual Bypass can offer a kind of mental-emotional salve, it actually *prevents* us from resolving old wounds.

In 2010, Robert Augustus Masters, PhD developed Welwood's ideas in his book, *Spiritual Bypassing: When Spirituality Disconnects us from What Really Matters.*[10] Masters summarizes the problem succinctly:

> *"Spiritual bypassing—the use of spiritual beliefs to avoid dealing with painful feelings, unresolved wounds, and developmental needs—is so pervasive that it goes largely unnoticed. The spiritual ideals of any tradition, whether Christian commandments or Buddhist precepts, can provide easy justification for practitioners to duck uncomfortable feelings in favor of more seemingly enlightened activity. When split off from fundamental psychological needs, such actions often do much more harm than good."*

What does this have to do with running your business? Well, maybe nothing, and maybe a lot. Here are just four examples of how holistic business folks can fall back on Spiritual Bypassing as a way to avoid learning how to run a business.

- *"If it was meant to be, my business would have succeeded. I guess (god, goddess, spirit) has something else in mind for me."*
- *"I must be burning off karma, which is why things just don't seem to work out for me."*
- *"I'm not allowed to charge for my healing service."*
- *"I run my business solely on love offerings."*

---

[10] Masters, Robert Augustus PhD. *Spiritual Bypassing: When Spirituality Disconnects us from What Really Matters.* North Atlantic Books. Berkeley, CA 2010.

These, and many more, are misguided notions about the inter-relationship between money, service, and success. It's painful to watch and pointless to take on. In the end, you simply cannot be of true service if your life is a continual struggle.

There is no big vindictive God in the sky who says you can't have abundance, or that you must burn off karma and live in poverty, or that you are not permitted to thrive doing what you love ... or any other similar notion.

ༀༀ

"You simply cannot be of true service if your life is a continual struggle."

ༀༀ

You were meant to thrive. And if the Universe/God/Divine had the wherewithal to seed a dream within you, it most certainly has the abundance to provide you with it.

But you have to be a part of that creation. We cannot sit passively by and wait for our angels to bring forth dense, material results. It's up to us to take action toward our dreams, develop the skills necessary to operate in a physical economy, value our time and skills, then position ourselves to both serve and thrive.

There is an old Christian saying which makes simple sense of this point: "The Lord Helps Those Who Help Themselves." And this begins with a change in mindset.

Formula for Failure

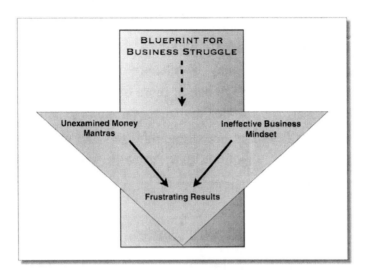

A toxic money blueprint begins with outdated beliefs about money. This is often reinforced with Spiritual Bypass and affects your thoughts, behaviors, and actions, including how you structure your fees. This, in turn, leads to ineffective business mindsets and their companions — unexamined money mantras. The results are inevitable — frustratingly low income.

After awhile, these patterns are ingrained in your psyche and this becomes an acceptable way of life. Soon you are living out of whack. Your energy is being drained and nothing is coming in — few sales, little money, diminishing optimism or energy. You may even compromise your values just to "get by." Poor results reinforce those ineffective mindsets and unexamined mantras, and so the cycle continues.

This blueprint has got to go. As long as you live in a state of energetic debit — with more energy going out than what's coming back to you (yes, in the form of money) — then you don't have the power you'll need to make a difference in the world. If you are letting yourself be chronically underpaid for the valuable services you offer, then it's up to you, and only you, to CHOOSE change.

Let's break down this Toxic Blueprint. First, I'm going to describe four typical, ineffective business mindsets that are a sure-fire set-up for struggle. Although it may be uncomfortable to accept, you'll probably recognize yourself in one or more of these. Then I'll explain how these mindsets support and are supported by unexamined money mantras. Then we'll look at how these mindsets and mantras guarantee frustrating results. Finally, in Part IV we'll explore how you can reframe your beliefs and actions in order to:

√ **Do what you Love**
√ **Make a Difference**
√ **Thrive!**

Chapter Seven
Ineffective (Business) Mindsets

Ineffective Mindset #1 — The Hobbyist

If your work in the world is of service to the greater good, yet you're struggling just to make ends meet, maybe you need a little "anger therapy" to recognize a Hobbyist Mindset ...

My Angry 'Aha!'

For me, the Hobbyist Mindset hit home HARD when a business acquaintance called looking for a quick turn-around on a copywriting job to promote her new program. No problem. I don't *love* quick turn-arounds, but hey, I understand being in a pinch too. Then she dropped the verbal equivalent of a bomb on me — "I need it done on a tight budget."

Why was this a *bomb*? Because she wanted me to drop my other work, put hers at the head of the queue so that she could more effectively promote her program (read: make more money), and then under-pay me for it. She knew I had more than a decade of experience as a professional writer and was a well-trained marketing strategist. To be blunt, she was basically saying, "I'll pay a pittance for your expertise, so that I can increase my income."

Let's translate this to your experience:

√ You've spent many years mastering your skills.
√ You've invested 1000s, if not tens of thousands of dollars for proper training, certifications and experience.
√ You are now really awesome at what you do. Yet ...

You've got the whacky notion that you should only charge $20 or $40 or $60 bucks an hour for what you do — or worse, a love offering.

Sorry, but does this make even a little sense to you? Logically, this kind of thinking is full of holes. But it continues because so many of us have been duped into believing one of two things:

1. Our life-transforming services are less valuable than, say a new carburetor in your car, a trip to the Bahamas, or a daily latte. Or ...

2. Our services are so precious that we are obligated to practically GIVE THEM AWAY to folks who can't appreciate them enough to drum up cash to pay for them (even if they can sort out what they need for a night on the town or a new outfit).

An Anger that Heals?

The anger that rose in me when I read my friend's request shocked me. It also changed my life. To be clear, my anger wasn't at her. Not at all! It was with myself, for willingly broadcasting an energy that said, "I am an expert and I'll accept crumbs in order to help you live a better life."

This 'Aha!' rocked my world in a good way and helped me understand the message I now share with healers, teachers, and anyone who is under-charging for their valuable services. And what is that message? Plain-n-simple: **Honor your work as more than a hobby and charge what your expertise is worth.**

Ineffective Mindset #2 — The Holy Broke Helper

At this point, if you're feeling uncomfortable with what I'm sharing, you might be thinking something like, "But Dawn, remember that line in the bible! 'it's easier for a camel to get through the eye of a needle' ... ?"

Context, my friend. Context.

This message was delivered to those under the yoke of the Roman Empire. (And yes, the parallel with the Multinational Corporate Empire of today has not escaped me.) But the percentage and behavior of the wealthy in those times was quite different than today.

The dispossessed (*les miserables*) throughout most of patriarchal history have been treated worse than animals. Marie Antoinette's famous line, *"Ils mangent la brioche,"* illustrates her complete removal from the reality of the world all around her. She was *clueless* to the fact that people were starving in the streets. So when she was told that the people were rising up because they didn't have any bread to eat, her response was that of the cosseted child she was: "well then, let them eat cake!"

When you think about such a history — wealthy money changers, god-like royalty, exploitative land barons, rapacious tax collectors and chronically indentured servitude — it's easy to connect wealth with corruption. But we don't live in such a world as that anymore. Not all of us anyway. As privileged westerners we have every opportunity to live in abundance and leverage that kind of peace and plenty to better the world around us.

Aristocrats leaching off the masses, generally didn't do things that Conscious Wealth Creators today are doing. Things like:

- Practicing the healing arts to help others while vitally sustaining themselves.
- Writing books to educate and inspire.
- Hosting TV shows and getting corporations to sponsor gifts and tangible aid to thousands of needy people.
- Creating publishing companies to spread new thought.
- Starting foundations to help others get ahead.
- Micro-financing Third World women.
- Having PBS specials to educate and help others.
- Traveling the world delivering workshops and training that transforms lives.

So when it comes to that famed quote, "It's easier for a camel to go through the eye of a needle than it is for a rich man to get into heaven," I'm calling bull on this outdated notion of "holy broke" helping.

This old belief no longer serves the age in which we live. Stories, parables, myths and sometimes even morals are all about context after all, and when the Christ said this to a young wealthy man, the context was very different than that of today. Yet the notion that wealth and success are anathema to true service persists.

There are still too many good folks in the world today whose spiritual or religious beliefs are getting in the way of their greater potential to serve and succeed. And if you're reading this, there's a good chance that you, or someone very close to you, is one of them.

Despite the fact that we now have many exemplary role models for wild success and wealth who are moral, responsible, and in service to the greater good (think Oprah, Dr. Wayne Dyer, Louise Hay, Jack

Canfield, Deepak Chopra ...) too many are still just eking by, struggling to make ends meet, and having difficulty *receiving* the tremendous abundance which is the birthright for us *all*.

If you truly want to be of service, to live a life of purpose — free of the stress that comes from survival-mode living — yet a large part of your energy is spent juggling just to make ends meet, then I must ask you this: How well can you serve, uplift, and heal under these conditions? I know, this is a rhetorical question because the answer is obvious. The more you struggle with meeting your basic needs, the less time, energy, inspiration, and *money* you have to live a quality life and to help others.

Oh Those Impure Thoughts!

Here's a list of some of the false, (shall we say, impure?) beliefs many of us carry about money, service and success. All of these need to be given the heave-ho, once and for all. Have a look and then check in with yourself to see if any of these are operating in your belief system.

1. *"Rich people are greedy."*
2. *"The only way to really succeed is to step on other people's backs."*
3. *"Most success stories have a 'back story' of unhappiness and sacrifice."*
4. *"In order to make a lot of money I have to lie, cheat or compromise my values."*
5. *"I don't want to be selfish, so I'd better charge less."*
6. *"To be wealthy means I'll have to give up time that should be spent with family, in spiritual service or attending to my spiritual practice."*

7. *"Why should I enjoy the good things in life when there are starving children in Africa?"*

8. *"The love of money is the root of all evil."*

9. *"Money can't buy happiness (and therefore I should not pay attention to it)."*

10. *"Money isn't important to me."*

If any of these sneaky thoughts are still lurking around in your psyche, I strongly urge you to bring them to the light, explore if and how they may have served you in the past, and then *free yourself* from them at your earliest convenience. In the questions at the end of this section you'll find an exercise you can use to facilitate this process.

In the meantime, let's come at this in a purely practical way. Imagine someone whose business is struggling. They're working hard, but the customers and cash aren't flowing in. They must operate therefore, under a tight budget. Now, keep in mind that "tight budget" often equates to a *lot more* DIY (Do It Yourself) in all areas of the business (and life!), and you can project ahead to the likely results — someone who must devote a lot of their business-building time (including education on how to run a business) doing non-business activities.

Here's just a few examples. I'm sure you can think of more.

- **Vehicle TLC.** When we live hand-to-mouth each month, a reliable vehicle may be a luxury we can't afford. Without one? Expect periodic jury-rigging, time and money-wasting repair work for that clunker.

- **Stop-Gap Income Boosters.** Second jobs? Third? How many extra hours do you need to pay the bills, invest in business growth, and save? How many months or years will you want to keep up that pace?

- **Just-in-Time Bill-Paying.** Scrambling to get money into your bank before it hits an overdraft is a regular ritual for many business strugglers.
- **DIY.** Doing all the little tedious parts of your business yourself (instead of practicing your expertise) because you can't afford to hire an assistant.
- **Extra Work.** Living with shoddy appliances and furniture, or in a shoddy house that constantly needs repairs.

All of these and many more are complete time-wasters. When you first begin your business, some of these non-business activities, such as stretching the life of your car or taking a part-time job, can be a compromise worth making. It's an investment in your business. But at some point, when you come to realize that the one thing you can never ever get back in your life is time, you'll need to revisit this approach. In other words, you'll have to charge enough to live well and to outsource all the things you have no *business* doing yourself.

In order for you to serve in this world in the best way possible, you've got to be free of the constraints, hassles, and stress of just getting by. You have to take care of yourself and your material, physical needs. As they say on airplanes — "Please put your own oxygen mask on first before assisting others." Because in the end, the more time you waste doing everything else, the less time you have to actually *do* your good work in the world.

When faced with chronic financial and time burdens, we are the ones who are much more likely to compromise our morals. Because when we live in true abundance — which includes financial prosperity — we don't need to resort to certain *questionable* coping strategies.

I'm not suggesting outright stealing, murder, mayhem, or other nasties. I'm talking about the many subtle approaches to skimming and "fudging." Consider the following scenarios and ask yourself if you've ever considered (or done) something similar.

- I knew someone who, in order to get a little extra insurance money to make ends meet, had a friend drive his old beater car several states away and abandon it on a remote dirt road. The car owner then put in a claim that it had been stolen, and received enough cash to buy a much better car.
- I've known of several people who will go to a restaurant and at the end of the meal complain enough to get their meal for free.
- How about all the fathers who hide income so they can pay less to the mothers of their children (and these days, vice versa!)?
- Then there's the health compromises, like buying poor quality food because it's cheaper, or getting on Medicaid because actually dealing with our illness through nutrition or alternative health care is too expensive.
- Buying cheap crap made in sweat shops by children ... another area most of us are willing to overlook with the simple justification that "I can't afford the high quality, fair trade stuff."

With high values and high purpose, financial prosperity supports you and expands the good you do.

So while it may seem on first blush that integrity and wealth are anathema, when we dig a little deeper it's easy to see the error in this argument. An abundance of money is the vehicle by which you are able to be and do more in the world. With high values and high purpose, financial prosperity supports you and expands the good you do.

Ineffective Mindset #3: The Passive Attractor

Many of us begin our journey into business with a heartfelt vision. Rather than being a cog in the wheel of a corporation, or opening a business simply to fill a need in the marketplace, we want to help. We want to bring value to others and we want to combine our skills with a higher calling. In other words, we want to align our work with our Soul Purpose. In fact, it's clear that at this juncture in history, many of us are being called to be of high service in this way.

This is, after all, the "dawning of the age of Aquarius," so it's no surprise that many are opting out of traditional forms of work or career in order to build something new. With great enthusiasm and joy we throw ourselves into developing the skill sets we need. We work hard cultivating mastery, gaining knowledge, growing personally, re-awakening our personal power. Sometimes there are challenges, but our Soul Purpose Calling seems to pull us forward through the obstacles.

In time, we pass the tests, gain the certifications, and hang the joy-fully-earned 'shingle' in our community. And then comes, for many of us, the reality check — getting clients and customers.

Screech! Whoa! Wait a minute! Nobody told me I had to actually sell myself and my services in order to make the business, um ... work.

Action: The Other Part of the Equation

The unconquerable obstacle for many Holistic Business Owners comes when it's time to promote and SELL what we do. Sure, we take action, but it's all related to skill building for the services we offer.

Unfortunately, this is only half of the equation. Without taking action in the direction of building a business (read: marketing and selling), there will be no growth. The cold hard truth is this — if you are in business, you must take action on both sides of the Equation — your Mastery and your Business.

This is particularly challenging for those of us who recognize the power and truth of the Law of Attraction. We believe that "If I build it, they will come because my *intention* will attract them." Unfortunately, this isn't exactly how the Law of Attraction works. We attract based on our energies. So if you want to run a *business* you have be in an energy-state that supports your business — by taking *business-related actions.* In other words, you must treat your business like a business, not like a hobby (see Ineffective Mindset #1 for further details).

What does this mean? It means marketing. It means sales. It means charging a fee that supports you. And it means asking for the sale. Beyond that, it means all the things necessary for a business to be ... a business.

There are two primary reasons why many of us avoid action connected with sales and marketing. The first is obvious, it's the vision. The healing, wholing, transformative service you want to offer which inspired you and set you on your path to business — not *the selling and promoting* of that service.

The second is a bit more complex, and it has to do with our mindset around marketing and sales. Let's face it, many elements of mainstream society have left a bad taste in the mouths of those seeking authentic purpose. When marketing becomes a highly refined strategy for stuffing more high fructose corn syrup, GMO junk, and toxic dyes into our children, who wouldn't be suspicious of business marketing?

Add to this the natural abhorrence many of us feel for mega-sized corporate consumption, is it any wonder that we just want to return to a grass-roots way of living and working? Is it any wonder that many of us feel called to serve our communities, seeking greater connection to the value of the small, the holistic ... the real?

The world has gotten awfully large, and as Mother Theresa once said, *it's those small acts done with great care which can truly make a difference.* The problem is that we throw the baby out with the bath-water. Instead of exploring how we can use the best parts of market-ing and sales in order to reach, serve, and facilitate transformation in more people, we avoid or reject any sales efforts all together.

When we write off all marketing as sleazy, all sales conversations as pushy, and all business promotion strategies as *marketeering* we undermine our capacity to reach and serve others. This attitude is the death knell for your business, particularly in our new, digitally connected world. When you avoid building a strategic marketing plan, you lose the opportunity to actually reach the people you most want to serve. And when you don't learn how to have a sales conversation? Cash flow trickles and eventually runs dry.

Here's an example of the consequences of not activating the mar-keting and sales arm of our businesses.

Yoga: An Idea Before it's Time? ... Not!

Several years ago, in a pretty hip college town, someone opened a small yoga studio. A few students trickled in from time to time. The business limped along. The conclusion of the studio owner after several months? "I guess this town just isn't ready for a yoga studio."

Not long after said studio owner drew this conclusion, a friend and colleague (also a yoga teacher), decided that just couldn't be true. This was, after all, the 21st century in an American university town, complete with crystal shops, new age book stores, and groovy coffee houses.

My friend, also a well-trained marketer, decided to host a yoga festival in this same town. The results? Locals came out of the wood-work, money-in-hand, to attend! The Festival went on to attract people from around the nation, becoming a highly desirable, annual gig for many yoga teachers.

Yoga was, in fact, wanted in this hip college town. The problem was that the yoga studio owner mentioned above didn't have a marketing plan to turn what she had built into an actual business. She built it, but no one came.

She was being passive about growing her business. She had no marketing strategy, little or no money budgeted for marketing or business training, and therefore no understanding of which actions to take. Now I'm not saying flyers in cafes are a bad idea per se, but I am saying they're an exceedingly poor alternative to employing a *Marketing Plan* (including leveraging the internet), that is proactive and strategic.

That progressive town was more than ready for a yoga studio. However, the idea to "build it and they will come" is a passive business plan. It's the tagline of a movie, not a marketing strategy.

I've devoted Chapter 9 entirely to Marketing and Sales. I strongly urge you to read through it carefully. In it you'll find an in-depth look at the reasons behind the discomfort many of us feel about these critical business skills, along with some easy, how-to skills you can develop to help bring your business and services to the people who need what you've got.

Ineffective Mindset #4: When Thrift Becomes A Vice

Thrift becomes a vice once it crosses over into tight-fisted penny-pinching. The Thrifty Mindset stems from a fear of debt. It manifests with those who attempt to build a business based on free — free advice, free webinars, free opt-in gifts, free support, and free, complimentary consultations.

These are the folks who accept tickets to free conferences but never join the programs offered. They jump on plenty of free webinars, schedule multiple complimentary consults to try and squeeze every last bit of advice out of business professionals, and opt into numerous free downloads, but never actually invest in a full program or business support. These are the folks who waste their own time and everyone else's. It's a silly way to try and build a business.

Here are two reasons why a excessive thrift will never serve a true business builder.

1. It's an energetic mismatch. In other words, you get what you pay for — nothing. No one can grow a successful business without investment in the business. So if you were hoping to build a business without spending any money on business growth, (beyond certifications, supplies, and overhead) you are thinking like an employee. Let's clear this up now — it won't work.

2.   When it comes to business building, FREE information is not *supposed* to give you everything you need. Free webinars, downloads, conference tickets, and consultations are designed for you to get a taste of the product, program or services of the provider so that you can invest in their support if it is what you need.

Now please understand, I'm not suggesting you stack up debt and spend wildly. Being cautious about debt is just smart business. But being unwilling to *leverage* debt in order to grow your business is a contraction-based decision.

There are times when we need to use credit and debt to invest and grow. Whether that's investing in equipment, assistance, coaching, or the cost of launching a new program, debt can actually serve you when used correctly.

But here's where many small business owners get stuck. They say to themselves, "when I make some money, I'll invest in support." The problem with this is that it doesn't work that way — on both a practical and energetic level.

Peter's Short-Sighted Thriftiness

Peter is a Life Coach. He's very good at what he does and thanks to his exposure as a tour guide in a tourist town, Peter consistently gets great prospects. Peter came to me because, like many solo service businesses, he wasn't making as much money as he would like.

We had a look at Peter's offerings and it was clear that there was a lot we could do to quickly increase his sales as a life coach and reduce his need to spend so many hours delivering tours each week.

Unfortunately, Peter had convinced himself that he could not afford to hire a marketing strategist. Why do I say "convinced himself?"

Because I know that Peter dines out regularly and is an avid spender on art and clothing.

Peter illustrates the profound short-sightedness of the Thrifty Mindset. He is now going about re-inventing the wheel of marketing, spending a lot of time, through trial on error, on things he may not need in hopes that he can pull off this marketing and sales stuff on his own.

What Peter (and so many other Holistic Business Owners) has been unable to hear is this — if he invests a few thousand dollars in strategic support, he'll be making *more* money very quickly — something a fine Italian dinner or a new turquoise belt will never do for him!

The Mirror Never Smiles First

Practically speaking, when you don't invest in what you need, you're much more likely to waste what money you do have by investing unwisely. Sadly, I see this again and again — Small business hopefuls throwing good money after bad instead of spending a little bit more on proper coaching, marketing, sales skills, or high quality equipment and supplies. When we choose to make no investment in growing our business until we make more money to do it, it's like saying to your reflection in the mirror, "I'll smile but you have to smile first." You'll wait a lifetime.

The flow of manifestation runs opposite to what we've been told. If you want to *manifest* something, you have to activate the energy first. This involves things like visualization and "acting as if ..." but it also involves *literal* action.

So the next time you find yourself saying something like, "I really need this for my business but I can't invest in it until I make the money from my business," take a good long look at whether this is true, whether you actually do have money you can reallocate or debt you can leverage, and whether or not the return on your investment has the potential to be worth it. Remember, the purpose of investing in your business is so that your business can grow, reach more people, and make money too.

My own Shift from Thrift

My own "shift" from a thrifty-to-a-fault mindset came when I attended my first conference for small business entrepreneurs.[11] At the time, I was beginning my third business. I was 47 years old, pretty much broke, and about 80% financially dependent on my boyfriend.

I had been given a free ticket to the event and, even though I had to spend some money to get there, I *really* wanted to make change. So I went.

To say I was uncomfortable for most of those pivotal three days would be an understatement. All of the issues of struggle I had been spinning around with for decades were hitting me in the face!

My hobby-like mindset about my business had been keeping me from actually learning how to run a business. And I saw how this was true even back in my martial arts years when I had $5000 worth of monthly overhead and 100+ students!

I was a Holy Broke Helper, with ideas about money that were absolutely *laden* with confusion and pain, then soothed through unexamined beliefs, and "spiritual bypass" habits of thought.

And while I had learned to at *least* take some marketing action, thanks to my Thrifty Miser approach to business, I had invested almost no money in real growth.

---

[11] Pamela Bruner's "Transform" event. Atlanta GA., Spring 2012.

Thankfully, something radically shifted for me during those three days. In retrospect I'd say it's because I was fed up enough to finally listen to someone who actually made it to where I wanted to be.

I was ready to break free of the struggle, no matter what.

To make a long story short, I made a dynamic and super scary move ... not knowing where the money would come from ... I committed to what seemed a very large sum of money at the time, for hands-on business coaching.

In fact, over the course of the next two years, I invested approximately $50,000 in mentorship, sales coaching, and business marketing in order to get OUT of struggle and IN to business success.

And it worked.

And it was scary. But here's what I discovered ... The Law of Attraction *does* work when you take appropriate action. Literally within 2 weeks of signing on the dotted line and committing to pay for the coaching I needed without having a *clue* where the cash would come from, I was offered an ongoing, retainer-based gig that paid for my investments!

When I smiled, the mirror smiled right back :)

Your "Shift"

Now I understand that your circumstances may be very different. After all, I didn't have small children at home and I *did* have a very supportive partner who could "hold down the fort" while I channeled most of my income into my business. So if my story were the exception, I wouldn't have bothered to share it with you here.

But my story is not the exception. There are many, many, many small business owners, service providers, and entrepreneurs who have their own version of the smiling first story. People just like you and me who didn't know where the money would come from, but who said "Yes" anyway in order to get the help they needed.

I'm not saying it's easy, because most of the time it isn't. I'm not saying some of us possess more courage, because we don't. (Personally, I was scared s**tless.) And I'm not saying that I or anyone can guarantee anything.

What I am saying is that if you genuinely want to make your Soul Purpose Calling an income-generating business, you must find a way to spend money to grow it.

Ensuring Struggle or Success?

These four Ineffective Mindsets —The Hobbyist, the Holy Broke Helper, the Attraction without Action, and the Thrifty — illustrate some of the most common mistakes we make when we try to build a business without a healthy money blueprint. All four will ensure struggle rather than success. Ultimately, these mindsets begin to poison our thinking and our actions, and inevitably have a negative impact on our lives.

As long as we are operating our business (or our lives for that matter) from a toxic mindset around money, we will continually shoot ourselves in the proverbial foot when it comes to our finances. Perhaps the most significant way we do this (besides how we spend the money we have) is by justifying our situation with Unexamined Money Mantras.

I've identified seven of these mantras. There are probably more. But let's have a look at each of these in turn, and then we'll reframe them in a way that will serve to empower and align you with your Money, your Service, and your Success.

Chapter Eight
Unexamined Money Mantras

Money. The "root of all evil" or system of exchange? Let's have a look now at the kinds of unexamined money mantras that arise when we dwell too long in toxic mindsets, and the customers aren't knocking on our doors.

In the end, your work in the world is about your service, it's about energy exchange, it's about choices, and it's about the money, isn't it? This is why I believe it's important for us to look at our unexamined money mantras and then reframe some of the negative ideas we have about cash.

We'll do this by identifying seven of the most common mantras, justifications, compromises, and spiritual by-pass habits of thought you'll find in a toxic money blueprint. Each of them is major foil if you truly want to serve because they are business killers.

So please, read through these carefully.

Unexamined Money Mantra #1:
"I can't afford to invest any more money in my business."

I wish I had a dime for every conversation I've had with a prospective client who genuinely needs my help as a consultant or copywriter, but cannot bring themselves to say "yes" because they "don't have the money."

It's an unexamined mantra for most. After all, I'm not talking with prospective clients who are living in homeless shelters or who are so financially strapped that daily survival is all they can manage. I'm talking about women and men who have businesses. Women and men who have earned, borrowed, or drummed up tens of thousands of dollars over the years to learn and master their skills, and then hang their shingle that says "open for business."

These are business owners who have all the skills they need to call themselves a pro and be successful, but then choose to come to a screeching halt when it's time to invest in the *business* of their business. The results are typical. They do all sorts of things they don't need to do, attempt to reinvent the wheel with everything from filing papers to website building, to bookkeeping, and they *don't* spend nearly the amount of time they need to doing the things that will actually make them money (read: sales, marketing and fulfillment)!

I did this myself for many years and over the course of two different businesses. It was exhausting and joyless.

Think about it. You've invested so much time, energy, money, and love into cultivating the modalities and skills you value. What good are you doing — yourself or the world — by keeping these wonderful tools in your proverbial tool belt? And the tool belt is exactly where your skills will stay if you don't invest in developing two additional critical skills. These are the skills that generate revenue: Marketing and Sales.

How much sense does it make to have invested in skill mastery and not be able to support yourself with it? The truth is, if you cannot bring yourself to invest in the business skills and strategies necessary to support yourself and your family with your expertise, what's the point? People aren't going to flock to your door for service if you haven't learned how to market and sell to them. Learning how to do it is the only way you'll be able to take those valuable tools out of your tool belt and actually *use them.*

So if you find yourself writing off opportunities for support with the unexamined mantra, "I don't have the money," I want to invite you to pause, examine if it's true, and consider where you might drum up the money for what you see your business needs.

When you know how to sell your services this is easy – sell more stuff, get the money. But you may also choose to leverage debt, partner with someone who invests in your business for a percentage of sales later, or simply borrow money for needed growth. How it happens is not as important as the power you will bring to your business when you examine a default setting (an "unexamined mantra") that you can't afford to invest in your business.

Six More Unexamined Money Mantras

In addition to the BIG one, there are at least six other common mantras we use when it comes to money — or lack thereof. Let's have a look ...

Unexamined Money Mantra #2:
"The 'Love' of Money."

Why would people love (or fear, or hate) money? Money is a system of exchange. By having plenty of it, you can live your life with a degree of freedom that you can't have without it.

But many *don't* have money, while a very few have it in excess. Does this imply something about how *good* people should relate to money? Does this unequal distribution of money suggest that because some have so little we all should live that way? Is my abundance taking away from others? Is it my *fault* that other peoples and nations live in poverty?

The answer to these questions is revealed in another question, "Do I have any power whatsoever to change another person's poverty by remaining broke myself?" When you look at it this way it becomes obvious, doesn't it? Making a vow of poverty does not relieve anyone else of being broke. In fact, the opposite is true.

The poorest people in a wealthy western country buy the cheapest products. Products (like clothes, food, home furnishings) that are much more likely to be made in horrifically oppressive sweat shops by people who work under slave-like conditions and are some of the most impoverished people on the planet! It is only when we have money that we can invest in fair trade products, organic food, locally grown, and built stuff.

Unexamined Money Mantra #3:
"Money Can't Buy Happiness."

Freedom and happiness aren't exactly the same thing, but it's awfully hard to have happiness without a modicum of freedom. And in order to have freedom in a cash-based economy, you're going to need, *yep* ... MONEY.

In a world where the manufacturers and purveyors of *stuff* compete in an open market, and marketers meet their own bottom lines by strategies to get their clients more cash, we find ourselves in a world where *stuff* is equated with happiness and getting more *stuff* (right until you're in debt up to your ears) brings ultimate fulfillment. Of course this is nonsense. And those of us who know better shake our heads at the suffering too many who've succumbed to this capitalist coup now endure.

Most of us learn eventually that *stuff* will never lead to happiness, and acquiring more stuff will lead to enslavement, not freedom, no matter how much money you earn. What does all this have to do with the myth that the love of money is the root of all evil? Stay with me here while I explain.

When we get caught up in the story of *stuff* and lost in the black hole of debt, it's incredibly easy to allow the devils of our darker nature to take charge. The result of buying stuff for happiness is inevitable — powerlessness and enslavement to whatever it takes to pay for what we've got. In this sense, 'loving' money is more like a kind of dependent worship, not love. There's just no denying that this is a rotten way to go through life. Financial strain leads to stress, anxiety and too often, compromised moral choices.

From the outside, it looks like those who love money (read: are enslaved to consuming stuff for a down-graded sense of happiness), are often the ones willing to do the nastiest things in order to get more of it. But when we love the choices and freedoms that money can provide us with in order to live whole healthy lives; and the ability to donate and contribute generously to people and causes we believe in, then we are in alignment with this system of exchange, rendering the whole equation of money and evil irrelevant.

Unexamined Money Mantra #4:
"I've got to keep my prices really low or no one will be able to afford me."

Any great sales person will tell you one thing when it comes to price objections — "It's never about the money." Really, it never is. With rare exceptions, when someone doesn't have the money for your products or services, it's because they are not choosing to make what you offer enough of a priority to find the money or invest some of the money they've got.

The reason someone tells you that they don't want to buy what you are selling, is not likely because they can't afford it, but because:

- It's not a real match for what they need.
- They don't recognize the value of what it is you have to offer.
- They don't want to prioritize your offer because of a block or resistance they have about making change.

The first possibility is easy to deal with. You sell yellow widgits and I need blue thing-a-ma-bobs. You could have the best yellow widgits in the world and be the most authentic and astute salesperson in the world, but what you've got isn't a match for what I need. "Peace out!" as they say.

The second possibility places the onus on you, the seller, to clarify the value of what you are selling to your prospect. It's not your prospect's job to intuit the benefits. It's not their job to understand or assume how your services will help them, or be wowed by you based on your credentials. As business owners, it's each and every one of our responsibilities to *communicate the value of our offers in a way that our ideal prospects and clients will understand.*

I realize this may make you feel uncomfortable. I realize the implication here — that it's your job to sell; and I realize that you may not like this too much, but the bottom line is the success or failure of your business is indeed, your responsibility. And that means ... *sales.*

The third possibility is about their mindset related to change. This can be a tough one to deal with if you have not been trained in the skills of effective sales (see Chapter 9 for starter tips).

You see, sometimes we can see possibilities for our prospective clients that are way bigger, brighter, and more magnificent than they can see for themselves. Often, we can also see the opposite side of that coin: the negative results of their not taking positive action toward change.

But the human ego is a funny thing. Even when its self-identity is causing great pain, the possibility of change can appear far more threatening. When you are making an offer to someone whose opposition to investing is a resistance to change, small is in order. Be their Advocate by helping them to see a few of the small positive changes (rather than the big potential vision) that will be possible when they say "Yes!"

Unexamined Money Mantra #5:
"I Don't Care About the Money."

Most, if not all Holistic Business Owners are very clear about at least this — we want to help. We want to do good in the world and make a positive difference in our communities, for our clients, or for the world. This is a genuine drive among an ever-increasing percentage of the population, and it's a very good thing indeed!

But because money is such a big *bugaboo*, those of us who have a mission to serve like to imagine that what we do is not about the money. And so we say things like, "I do this for the love of it; I don't care about the money." Or, "I don't want to get rich or anything, I just need enough to get by."

In one sense this is absolutely true. Those of us high enough on Maslow's scale of needs to actually heed the call of our Soul Purpose work in the world, genuinely *want* to do our good work for the benefit of all. It's not about the money, it's about the service.

The problem is, if we cling to the belief that it's not about the money, without grounding our service in the market economy in which we live, we can easily spiral downward into giving without receiving — giving from an empty vessel.

There's no win in this kind of giving, because there is no equal exchange of energy. It's like exhaling repeatedly without ever inhaling. It just doesn't make sense. The results are predictable.

- Cycles of burn-out
- Very few people actually served
- Business failure

In the bigger context of the material plane where we are living and growing a business, if you don't make it about the money, you won't have the capacity to truly serve.

Unexamined Money Mantra #6:
"It's So Expensive!"

This Mantra is really about values and priorities. Because here's the bottom line: Whatever it is we value, we find the money for it. Every time. How many financially struggling yoginis, massage therapists, and energy healers will come up with the two, three, or even ten grand needed for another training, certification, or retreat? Plenty.

How many BhaktiFest or Burning Man attendees will move mountains to purchase their annual tickets, but otherwise can't rub two dimes together when it comes to actually creating financial stability for their lives? And how many otherwise financially struggling people still buy those four dollar lattes a few times a week, go out to restaurants, or have after work drinks at the local pub?

Justifications for Under-Charging

I used to live in a small, seasonal tourist town. Most of the folks who live there full time are in one kind of service industry or another. They ride a roller coaster with their incomes from boom-to-bust, twice annually. Far too many of them, sadly, have habits of thought, word, and deed which make that roller coaster all the more nauseating. They undercharge during low seasons and undercharge locals throughout the year. Why? Because, as one massage therapist acquaintance once pronounced, garnering nods from the group of local healers she was speaking to, "*nobody* has any money in this town."

But in a community loaded with multi-million-dollar second and third homes, a luxury ski resort and millions spent by tourists annually, this mantra is little more than a myth — albeit a potent one. Why do I say this with such confidence? Because many of the supposedly 'broke locals' spend their low seasons doing things like going on month-long vacations to exotic lands, bellying up at the local bar regularly, or drinking four-dollar lattes most mornings.

Broke? I don't think so.

"Expensive" is a perception. It's not about the price point, but about perceived value. I believe this is a major reason why many heart-centered business owners, service providers, and artists are deeply uncomfortable about charging based on the value of our services and products.

Let's face it, it's painful to hear someone imply that our hard-earned mastery isn't valuable ... isn't "worth it." Ouch! So we must remember that "too expensive" is someone else's *perception* of our service or product — not our own intrinsic worth as a human or a professional.

Unexamined Money Mantra #7:
"I Can't Charge That Much!"

If charging an amount that will allow you to live well sounds like "too much," then it's time to ask yourself an extremely important question: Why are you trying to make a business out of something you cannot charge enough to live well and thrive by doing?

When it comes to this issue of charging "too much" there's another key question you'll want to ask as well. On what do you base your price? Others in your industry? A baseline price set by your community for your kinds of services? How much your friends or colleagues make? What you believe the market will bear?

If the thought of raising your prices runs through you like a cold steel blade, but what you're charging right now isn't enough for you to thrive (or maybe even survive!), you've got to address this head-on. If you don't, you're just postponing the inevitable.

It's important to look closely at several issues here. The first is the true value of the transformation your products or services offer. It's worth taking the time to consider the primary and tertiary benefits your services or products provide. Particularly in the service industries, it's easy to get caught up in a per-hour rate structure. But when you charge in this way, you neglect to take into account two other major parts of the equation:

1.   The time, money and energy you've invested in mastering the skills in the first place.
2.   The transformative value (the beneficial results) your services provided.

One of the best ways I've ever heard this articulated was by the highly successful business coach Pamela Bruner. As a long-time EFT tapper and co-author of a book on *Tapping Into Ultimate Success* with Jack Canfield, Pamela understands what it means to provide life-changing service. At one of her annual *Transform* events, she said something that radically improved my understanding of pricing. Paraphrased here, Pamela said,

> *There will always be bargain shoppers. People looking for the cheapest or best deal. But there will also always be those who want to be fully and completely cared for — those who want to invest in the highest quality services and products.*

These are people willing to pay for what I call *comprehensive transformation* or *holistic transformation*. They want the whole package. This is why every spa offers both a la carte services as well as deliciously bundled packages. There will be those who come to the spa with a budget for a 50-minute Swedish massage and those who want a full day extravaganza with massage and facial, sauna, steam bath, hot rocks, hot oil or whatever heavenly array of services the spa has to offer.

So if the prices you charge are not enough to support you, you've got to re-evaluate a few things. First, you have to determine whether your decision to run a business makes sense in light of the fact that you feel unable to charge a price that would let you live well. Second, you have to determine (if you do believe you have something of great value to offer) what you need to charge for the true value of the service and transformation you provide.

Finally, you need to decide on whom you are basing your pricing— the budget or *a la carte* shopper, or the client looking for a full package.

Your Money — Your Power

Your ability to command your life and serve others — in this world, at this time — is in direct proportion to your financial empowerment. This means the opposite is true as well. The more financially disempowered you are, the less able you'll be to empower other areas of your life.

From personal experience I can say with certainty, if you let yourself live too many years in material marginalization, you will be ...

- Far less able to manifest your sweetest dreams.
- At risk of facing financial panic if a serious health problem, major expense, or unexpected financial emergency arises.
- Much more likely to atrophy your "receiving muscles" for abundance.
- Likely to lose your understanding of how to flow money into your life.

When we keep ourselves too long in material struggle — even for seemingly noble reasons — we end up wasting our lives doing things that prevent us from doing the work we are here to do. They stymie our service and success. These include things like fixing clunker cars, taking on second, third or even fourth jobs just to make ends meet, figuring out your taxes yourself, doing repairs on home, vehicle or furnishings. These are all things that you should not be doing because they take you two, three, or even four times longer than hiring a professional to do them.

This is why it's so very important to look at any unexamined talk tracks or mantras you may have around investing in yourself and your business. Whether it's a default, "I don't have the money to invest in what my business needs" argument, one of the other six unexamined money mantras we've looked at in this chapter, or any others that keep you locked into a no-growth situation, holding onto these patterns of thought will never get you ahead.

There really is truth to the saying: "You have to spend money to make money."

Dawn DelVecchio

Chapter Nine
Marketing & Sales for the Holistic Business Owner

Sleazy, Pushy, Tacky and Rude! —
The Marketing and Sales Thought Glitch

How you market your business is an important part of your success, but it doesn't need to compromise your values. If you're a holistic business owner with clear values — and you're not strung over the financial barrel — then you answer to a very high ethical standard in your business and your life. In fact, most small business owners who are in service have impeccable integrity when it comes to their clients, customers, brand promise, and business dealings. This is part-and-parcel to the new world to which we all contribute, a world based on justice, balance and enough for everyone.

But there's a glitch in thinking for many of us when it comes to actually promoting our businesses, and making a viable, thriving living. It's confusion around marketing and it needs to be cleared up.

Most of us grew up exposed to advertising messages that were foisted upon us. Whether it was 'Joe Camel' on billboards (remember those?) or obnoxiously repetitive TV commercials, we've been solicited to by companies making big promises, peddling stuff we don't want, and quite frankly, most of us are sick of it. Not only are we sick of it, when it comes to our own businesses, the last thing we want to do is *that*. This is when our thought glitch surfaces, and we confuse marketing with tacky self-promotion.

It's unfortunate how much resistance there is around marketing among holistically-oriented business owners, particularly those in the healing and energy work fields. When I mention a pro-active marketing plan to some, they respond to me as if I have just suggested they start whoring themselves on a street corner!

Marketing does not need to be sleazy. It does not require being pushy, making false promises, exaggeration or spamming people. In fact, successful marketing in the age of the internet requires the exact opposite. After all, what's so *dirty* about informing the public who you are, what you do, and the benefits that your services provide? Nor do you lower your standards by telling people the solutions or transformation you offer, even if you sing it from virtual rooftops or send it to their inbox. If you want to actually *help* people, it's your *obligation* to inform them about these things.

Consider Coca Cola. From New York to Hong Kong, London to Sydney, everyone knows Coke. But their brand super-stardom doesn't mean they rest on their marketing laurels. In fact, according to *Business Insider*[12] Coca Cola spends more on advertising annually ($2.9 billion) than Microsoft and Apple combined!

My point here is not to use Coke as a role model for best marketing practices. It's simply to point out that marketing and sales are essential to *any* business, even the biggest, most well-known companies in the world.

So, if you have a tendency to equate the word "marketing" with things like sleazy, pushy, tacky, or rude, I want to invite you to reframe this in a new way. Yes indeed, there are plenty of examples out there of "sleazy, pushy, tacky, and rude" marketing. But! There is another thing called good marketing, and here's what it can do.

---

[12] http://www.businessinsider.com/facts-about-coca-cola-2011-6?op=1

- **Good marketing informs.** It offers high-value information in order to help consumers make choices.
- **Good marketing is personalized.** It tells your authentic story in a way that helps consumers do their own homework about what they need and with whom they would like to work.
- **Good marketing engages**. It helps people get in touch with what they really want and the discomfort necessary to help them make change.
- **Good marketing is simply good business.**

The Pain of Selling

Many Holistic Business Owners don't want to have to deal with the whole money-sales-pricing conversation. As I've already mentioned, some of us are deeply uncomfortable with our own pain around money, and so we can't deal with charging enough or having these conversations with others. The results are consistent at least — chronic struggle.

When you carry this vibration of discomfort about the money thing, it is felt by your prospects and clients subconsciously. This sets you up for a kind of vicious cycle of attracting people who either a) don't value what you do; or b) genuinely don't have the money for your services.

Addressing the issue head-on is the only way to change it. This means learning the skills necessary to value your services properly, and then selling those services through sales conversations with prospective clients. Bottom line? You've got to learn sales skills. But before you can take on these skill sets, the first thing you need to do is clear out any false beliefs about selling. What it is ... and what it isn't!

There's an erroneous association between selling and being pushy. Genuine selling, and asking for the sale, when done with authenticity and heart, has nothing whatsoever to do with being pushy. Think about it. If you have something of value to offer, something that can be of genuine service to the person you are speaking with, then why on earth would it seem pushy to ask them for the sale?

The Transference of Trust — One More Look at Selling

Selling is a very special kind of skill. One definition of sales is "the transference of trust." And a great sales person does this well. Sadly, many of us are suspicious of the sales process, believing it to be something sleazy and underhanded.

I'm not sure exactly where this came from, but I think there is an archetypal, used-car salesman skulking around deep within most of our psyches. You know the one — he's wearing a polyester leisure suit with the reverse seams. He's trying to hide his rather significant bald spot with a wet look comb-over, and he's offering you a lemon for the price of a Cadillac! That salesman image may have tainted our trust, but when we relax a little and choose to get some education around the sales process, a whole new awareness of what sales is — and what it can be — emerges.

We're going to have a look at selling from a different perspective. A perspective which will help you reframe selling entirely. First, I want you to take a moment to think about what you do. Are you good at it? Has it helped others?

Assuming your answers to these questions are yes, my next questions are:

- How much time and money have you invested to develop these skills?
- Did you get a degree or certification? (or two or three!)
- How much did that cost?
- Have the trials and errors of your experience brought you to a level of competence or even mastery?
- Do you have overhead?

Consider these questions carefully. They are fundamental to the way you value what you do, trust what you do and then transfer that trust to your prospects.

Your investment of time, money, love, and effort has tremendous value. If you agree, but you are having trouble with the sales conversation, what's going on? If what you do helps and serves others, if it is something you've deeply invested your life in mastering, then why would you feel there is something wrong with asking to be paid for it?

I'd Rather Have a Root Canal!

Check in with yourself to pinpoint the root of your aversion to sales. You may be very clear, or you may just feel uncomfortable. If it is more of a feeling than a set of reasons, perhaps you've had a bad experience with scam artists in the past, and now you associate that with sales.

But maybe you haven't had bad experiences at all. Maybe you're just uncomfortable asking for money. If that's the case, there's a good chance you simply need to *learn* how to sell.

Selling is an art form. Yes, you read that right, an art form. Since selling is about transferring trust to your prospect — about yourself and your services — a great sales person is a caring person. A great sales person knows how to identify the prospect's problem and how to fix it by making a solid offer to help, and to do it in a way that makes the sale.

If you find the idea of selling so dreadful that you'd rather have a root canal, I strongly urge you to reconsider owning your own business.

You simply cannot run a business and avoid selling. If this truth gets you down, have hope! There are some incredible sales coaches out there who can help you with the sales conversation. Without this ability, you really cannot help the people you want to help.

You can talk yourself into believing your gifts, your authenticity, and word-of-mouth will be enough to get clients knocking down your door, but with rare exceptions, this is little more than wishful thinking. (If you've been in business for awhile and customers aren't knocking down your door, then you've got all the evidence you need.)

It's not within the scope of this book to cover sales skills. There are many trainers and experts out there who can help you with this core business competency. But, in order to give you a better framework for understanding what actually constitutes selling, there are a few points I'd like to share with you. This will help dispel the myth about sales as an act of aggression or inconsiderate pushiness.

Sales Skills Basics

In order to sell effectively, you will want to understand these four elements of effective sales:

1. Asking for the Sale
2. Overcoming Objections
3. Being an Advocate for your Prospect
4. Facilitating a Decision

Let's have a look at each of these to see how very much they are connected with authentic service.

1. Asking for the Sale

Believe it or not, people will not assume you are offering something unless you tell them you are, and then ask them to buy it. Assuming that people will just automatically pull out their wallet without you asking them, "Would you like to work with me?" or "When would you like to start?" or "How would you like to pay?" is a false assumption. You must make it clear and evident that you are inviting them to invest in your product or service. To put it plainly, if you don't ask for the sale, you'll rarely get it.

2. Addressing Objections

Objections aren't something to avoid. They're something to expect. You read that right. You should *expect* to face objections when engaged in a sales conversation. If this is a revelation to you, don't feel bad, it was for me too, and most folks I've come across who weren't raised by sales professionals.

In truth, you should welcome objections, because it means that your prospect is engaged enough with the *possibility of what you are offering* to make an objection in the first place. In other words, they're still in the conversation if they are raising objections! They just need more information or help with their decision. After all, if they just straight out say, "no thanks" (which is also a good thing, as you'll soon see), then you have no more room to clarify questions or concerns they may have.

When a prospect has objections, concerns, or doubts about your offer, this gives you the opportunity to really listen to what they need and demonstrate how you can help them.

Objections are normal. Objections are healthy. We all want to be sure we are investing in the right support, item, or solution. You can help a prospect solve their problem by having an open conversation about their objections and addressing their concerns.

3. Being an Advocate for your Prospect

An advocate? Am I not attempting to convince the prospect to buy from me? The answer to that question is unequivocally, absolutely, and positively *not*. If you see your prospect as your opponent whose mind you must change, you are in quicksand, not a sales conversation!

Remember, you are in service to help your prospects solve a problem, overcome an obstacle, gain something they need or get rid of something they don't need. You are a solution-provider and a problem-solver. The only time a sales conversation could possibly be oppositional is if you are trying to sell the wrong thing to the wrong person.

Again, when you recognize that you have the solution or support your prospect needs, but they are bringing up objections or concerns (about cost, timing, if it will really work, etc.), then it's your duty to be an advocate for them. Help them see how they can get the transformation they are seeking with you and your products or services.

It's a bizarre aspect of the human condition that we are sometimes more comfortable in our known *discomfort* than we are with change. (Hence the oft-quoted phrase: "Better the devil you know.") But when a person gets fed-up enough with the painful status quo of their lives, they begin to look for change.

When they find that opportunity for change in front of them — in the form of your hand reaching out to them with your offer — they can sometimes get cold feet. It is at this moment of the sales conversation when you have the opportunity to help them explore what their concerns are and find the way to a right decision for them. This is how to be an advocate for the transformation and solution they truly seek.

4. Facilitating a Decision

Just because you become their advocate, willingly taking on their objections with calm and clear responses, doesn't mean you are going to get a "Yes" from everyone. In fact, if you have a 20% "close rate" (meaning you close the sale for 20 of every 100 folks you speak with) you are doing quite well!

But getting a "Yes" isn't actually the goal of a sales conversation. The real goal of a sales conversation is helping your prospect make a decision. Again, if this comes as a surprise (or maybe even a shock), you're not alone. As I've said, a true Sales Master is an *advocate* for their prospect. She or he is someone with one goal in mind: Conclude every sales conversation with a clear decision by their prospect.

Why? Indecision, as one of my sales mentors, Suzanne Evans has rightly described it, is a form of self-torture. Indecision prolongs your situation. Indecision keeps you married to the problem. When you allow a prospect to leave a sales conversation without having made a decision, everyone is left in limbo. They haven't made a decision to change their situation, and you are now stuck following up, vaguely hoping that maybe they'll say yes. (Hint: they *rarely* do.) It's a losing situation for everyone.

When a prospect says "no," then you can both move on. The prospect can seek out a solution better suiting their needs (or stop vacillating about change they're not really willing to make), and you can move on to the next prospect.

Selling and Your Success

If you are uncomfortable with the sales conversation, I ask you to please sit with this discomfort for awhile. Explore it. Breathe into it a bit and truly *feel* what's going on for you around asking for the sale. This is important, because if you cannot stand in your integrity and ask for the sale — when you *know* that what you are offering can help the person you are speaking with — then you cannot run a successful business.

Getting clear about what the discomfort is will help you see through the confusion. Are you afraid of rejection? Afraid of other people accusing you of being pushy? Are you worried you might stumble over your words and not make the best presentation? What's going on about this for you?

If your business is struggling right now, it's no exaggeration to say that your ability to break through to better business income is directly related to your ability to let go of the false idea that asking for the sale is being pushy. So please, give yourself some time with this if it's triggering you. Then, get some sales training so that you can develop the skills you need to master this critical area of business.

Chapter Ten
Survival Mode — Consequences of a Toxic Money Blueprint

We've looked at ineffective business mindsets, unexamined money mantras and the importance of marketing and sales. Now it's time to have a look at the possible results you can expect from a toxic money blueprint: Survival Mode.

Survival Mode is the frustrating but likely result for Holistic Business Owners who have not healed harmful subconscious programming around money. It's the consequence and unfortunate situation many otherwise superb helpers, healers, teachers and leaders find themselves in.

Painful Justifications

When we permit our lives to go on, year after year, in financial struggle (or even, for some of you reading this, downright crisis) it twists the mind in a weird way. Inevitably this is supported by Spiritual Bypass. It becomes a source of comfort to think of money as something for the greedy, the unethical or the inauthentic masses. ("I may be broke and my life may suck a lot of the time, but hey, at least I'm a good person.")

It becomes a source of comfort to justify lack, with arguments that we are more clean or our intentions are more pure than those who know how to flow wealth into their lives. It becomes a source of comfort when anyone with wealth suffers a financial loss or gets screwed by banksters, gangsters or bad judgments. For some of us, it's even a kind of twisted comfort when our own situation worsens!

Whether it's buying 100% organic, raising our kids in great neighborhoods, living in a beautiful home, or generously giving to the causes we want to support, when we cannot avail ourselves of the quality of life we value, something is out of whack. Of course, those of us living outside the mainstream mindset can be highly tenacious. This includes plenty of creativity when it comes to turning lemons into lemonade.

Many of us spend decades managing chronic material struggle. The results can be impressive — inspiring, even! We figure out how to decorate with scraps of cloth, bulk trash furnishings and milk crates. We manage to sip lattes at trendy cafes even when we only make twelve dollars an hour. We get out in nature, make deep and lasting friendships, fix just about anything with a little duct tape and string, and most of the time, figure out how to get that last bill paid with five bucks to spare.

Tenacious? Absolutely! A model for making positive change in the world? No way.

When a large portion of your energy is spent in survival mode, no matter how creative, tenacious, inspiring and gifted you are, your chances of making an actual impact in the world are pretty slim. Add a few dependents, some debt or a little emotional drama to the mix? Forget about it. You'll be up to your ears in your own stuff. Someone else will have to bring forth the next revolutionary idea that moves an awakening society forward.

When we continue to remain broke, no matter how sincere our intentions or high the rest of our vibrational field is, we are failing in our task to aid in the planetary transformation. I'm serious, and I'm not willing to handle this issue with kid gloves, because broke and struggling = BROKEN ... as in: requires fixing; *does not work*.

Yet the (often pervasive) air of righteousness among a large number of people attempting to live more conscious lives keeps us locked into struggle and unproductive Spiritual Bypass.

On the one hand, we seek more "abundance" or "prosperity," while on the other we're the first to stand in moral condemnation of the wealthy or of marketing and sales, or of business owners who are committed to success. It's as if somehow, if we don't come by that elusive *abundance* through a divine dispensation (rather than say, charging what our services are actually worth), then any wealth is dirty money.

ᏚᎥᏟᎡ

When a large portion of your energy is spent in survival mode, no matter how creative, tenacious, inspiring and gifted you are, your chances of making an actual impact in the world are pretty slim.

Those suffering the most in their longing for abundance — for freedom from chronic material struggle — are often, as we've seen, the first to deny the importance of money. As

ᏚᎥᏟᎡ

if there is some invisible line which, when crossed, turns abundance into greed and prosperity into moral corruption.

No one's struggle is noble. And this is why business models (and I use that term loosely here) based on love offerings or a sliding scale, or a price range that will not ever make for prosperity — are not solutions to the problem. These are crutches that prevent us from being big in the world at best, and compel us to inappropriate decisions about business, at worst.

This disconnect between money, service and success is a poison. It's neither noble nor righteous to be financially incapacitated. In fact, when we cling righteously to our financially meager existences, we get in our own way.

Corruption, Empowerment and Money

At this point, you may be thinking something like: "But Dawn, the current monetary system is corrupt!" Yes, this is true. There are a host of problems when it comes to money: our monetary system is no longer based on the gold standard; corporate personhood allows corporate greed to go unchecked; there is excess corruption at the top; and the outrageous unbalance in the distribution of wealth leaves tens of thousands nationwide and millions worldwide in utter destitution.

The system IS corrupt. Change IS necessary. The structures of our economics DO need an overhaul. But this is what I truly want you to hear: *These are macro issues of injustice which will not change simply because you undercharge for your services.* Or more simply put ...

The system is corrupt, but you are not.

So until we get you economically stabilized (and empowered) enough to make a genuine difference with your good work in the world, things aren't going to change all that much. In fact, if you are unable to claim your right to financial prosperity, you effectively stop yourself from really helping people.

Let's Talk Empowerment

We can all talk until we're blue in the face about empowerment as if it is solely some sort of internal, spiritual, human potential, self-actualization phenomenon. We can also talk about empowerment as it applies to our right of choice to do things like heal ourselves naturally, eat organic food, speak our minds, honor our sexual preferences, birth our children at home or embody our spirit through the religion of our choice.

I know. I spent thirty years "empowering" myself in all those ways and plenty more. But you know what? Despite spiritual, holistic, educational and even *martial* empowerment (as in martial arts) for thirty adult years I was impotent to command my life.

I lived hand-to-mouth, by necessity I often had to compromise my values (to say nothing of my dreams!) more times than I care to say. I've been dependent on and forced to comply with the decisions of abusive boyfriends, one stingy husband, bully employers, petty tyrant colleagues and unappreciative clients. I've eaten (and fed my child) low-quality food because I couldn't afford organic, and cooked food for him and myself on aluminum pans. I've been stuck in foreign lands over holidays when all I wanted was to be with family; neglected my health and avoided medical care when I needed it; was unable to put my kid through college; and turned away more opportunities than I care to remember because they required investments I didn't have.

I lived most of my life stuck in a cycle of poverty and I can tell you for certain that no matter how free I've been to speak my mind, pick my sexual partners, spiritual practices or shopping outlets, there has been little that's truly empowering about it!

In the end, none of those non-material forms of empowerment meant very much when I lived in chronic struggle, riding a roller coaster that had me creeping up a (rather small) financial hill — only to roll rapidly down into burnout, resentment and exhaustion on a cyclical basis.

To Live and Give Generously

True empowerment means you are supported in doing what you do in a way that lets you live and give generously. True empowerment means you get to live the sweet dream you hold for your own life and also be able to pass it forward.

Think about the kind of difference you can make in the world if you had an extra five-thousand dollars to micro-finance small, Third World business owners. Think about what kind of an impact an extra ten-thousand dollars could make if you built schools for refugees on the borders of war-torn countries. Imagine what having enough time and money could do if you spent a month annually volunteering at a clinic to educate people about their health.

You want to talk about *helping?* THIS is helping. Chronically undercharging for services and expertise, on the other hand, is not.

Tying it All Together

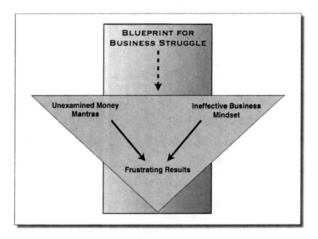

What I've described as ineffectual Business Mindsets, along with those Unexamined Money Mantras, arise when we hold on to outdated beliefs about money. The frustrating results are almost inevitable: struggle, or what I call "Survival Mode" living. I'm sure you'll agree that this is no way to go through life. Survival Mode benefits no one, least of all you.

Here are some exercises to help you uncover and examine any beliefs about business and money that may be undermining your ability to succeed, then determine what actions you will take to support you moving forward.

Please take your time with these — they're important for you, and for all the people whose lives may yet benefit thanks to your good work in the world.

EXERCISE 1: Examining Outdated Money Beliefs

The purpose of this exercise is to help you explore how well your internal conversation around money, service, and business success line up with each other.

This is best done with a journal and a relaxed mind. Using free association, and without stopping, list out as many answers as possible to each of the following lead statements.

1. Money is ...
2. When it comes to money, I ...
3. Selling is ...
4. Marketing is ...
5. When it comes to sales and marketing, I ...
6. My goals for my business are to ...

Once you've done the exercise, review your responses to see if there are any statements in numbers 1-5 that are misaligned with the statements you've written for number 6. Jot your insights down here or in your journal.

EXERCISE 2: Your Business Mindset

Of the four, Ineffective Business Mindsets we examined in Chapter 7, which, if any, do you relate to most? Make some notes under any of the Mindsets below about what you see differently now, and what actions you will take to "detoxify" yourself from behaviors related to these mindsets.

Ineffective Mindset #1: The Hobbyist

_____

_____

_____

_____

Ineffective Mindset #2: The Holy Broke Helper

_____

_____

_____

_____

Ineffective Mindset #3: The Passive Attractor

_____

_____

_____

_____

_____

Ineffective Mindset #4: The Thrifty Miser

_____

_____

_____

_____

_____

EXERCISE 3: Clarifying the Unexamined Money Mantras Holding Your Back

1. When it comes to investing in your business, what are the key phrases you tend to say (to yourself or others) when faced with a purchase decision? List them here or in your journal:

    1. _____

    2. _____

    3. _____

    4. _____

    5. _____

2. What have you been willing to spend money on for your business — without a second thought — before reading this book? (skill training, certifications, supplies, etc.)

    1. _____

    2. _____

    3. _____

    4. _____

    5. _____

3. What *might* you be willing to spend money on to grow your business, now that you've read most of this book?

1. _____

2. _____

3. _____

4. _____

5. _____

4. What kinds of business growth opportunities (mentorships or coaching, staff, home help, marketing support, sales training, etc.) have you never invested in? What price do you feel you may have paid for neglecting these?

Investment	Price you've "paid" for not investing

5. What are you willing to do to prioritize investing in your business in these new ways?

1. _____

2. _____

3. _____

4. _____

5. _____

6. What single *business* investment could radically up-level your business, if only you could afford it?

_____

7. When will you commit to investing in this? (Set a specific date).

_____

EXERCISE 4: Marketing & Sales

I've included a separate exercise for Marketing and Sales so that you can explore these critical elements of your business more deeply. For Holistic Business Owners who cannot seem to make ends meet, Marketing and Sales are the actions that are missing.

This exercise will let you brainstorm some ideas about how you will get support and begin taking action in these arenas.

Marketing

1. In order to accomplish the online and offline marketing strategies I wrote down at the end of Part II, I will need the following skills, training or support:

    a._____

    b._____

    c._____

    d._____

2. In order to get the support I need to effectively market and grow my business, I have allotted $ _____ (monthly/annually).

Sales

1. True or False: I love to sell! This is not a problem for me and I'm clear that in order to be of service, I must hold space and stand strong in sales conversations with my prospects.

2. True or False: Sales is a 4-letter-word! I don't like to sell and don't want to have to "sell" my services. The thought of having to hold sales conversations makes my stomach turn and my heart race! I'm hoping to get business by word of mouth, and the Law of Attraction, trusting that if someone is meant to be my client, they'll naturally gravitate to me and open their wallet willingly.

If you answered "True" to question #1, congratulations! In order to grow your business, reach and serve more people and thrive, you'll want to focus more on marketing and getting the word out about your business, so that you can hold more sales conversations.

If, however, you answered "True" to question #2, then it's essential that you put your focus on learning to sell *first*.

Here's why: If you cannot hold a sales conversation and stand strong in the face of objections or concerns by those who would benefit from your offer, then it doesn't matter how many people you reach with your marketing efforts (and precious dollars), it won't help. You must be able to sell if you want a successful business.

If you're feeling triggered right now, use your journal or the space below to write out whatever is coming up for you. If you use other modalities to reduce stress like EFT Tapping, meditation, deep breathing, primal scream therapy ... by all means, do that as well :)

When you feel complete with that, answer the following questions:

1. In order for me to be able to hold an effective[13] sales conversation, I am willing to hold _____ sales conversations each week. (Remember: a 20% conversion is doing really well. So if you want 2 new clients each week, consider a minimum of 10 sales conversations.)

2. In order for me to be able to hold an effective sales conversation, I am willing to invest in the following support (circle all that apply) ...
   a) Hire a Sales Coach. (*highly* recommended if you are terrified to sell!)
   b) Read a book on sales and practice the techniques.
   c) Take an online sales training course.
   d) Keep practicing! (This one is pretty much required ... sorry.)

3. In order to get the support I need to effectively sell my services, I have allotted $ _____ (monthly/annually).

---

[13] "Effective Sales Conversation" = Facilitating a *decision*. Sales conversations are not meant to convince, coerce or 'trick' people into buying what they don't want or don't need.

PART IV: A NEW CONVERSATION

Now that we've looked closely at the Spirit, Mind and Money of your business, you've probably got a very good sense of you business vision, your message, and your ideal client. Hopefully, you've also got specific marketing strategies you're beginning to implement. And of course, there's a good chance you've uncovered some beliefs, unexamined mantras, or "default" settings about money that you're now ready to release and transform.

In Part IV we're going to look at how to reframe outdated ideas about money. When you apply these reframes to your thoughts and conversations around money, they will help you to elevate your ability to have more money. This in turn will allow you to provide great service while enjoying real business success. In short, Part IV is where we set you up to apply what you've learned in Parts I-III so that you can thrive as a Holistic Business Owner!

Dawn DelVecchio

Chapter Eleven

Money, Service & Success: A New Conversation for Holistic Business Owners

The good news is that you can CHOOSE to stop living within a conversation about money that undermines business success. You can take actions that will break the cycle of struggle and the energetic debit that comes from giving with an empty vessel. **The remainder of the book is devoted to showing you how to ditch the ineffectual mindset around money, service and success, and take actions for change.** In it, we'll draw upon a more workable conversation for success. We'll also reframe the seven Unexamined Money Mantras that we use to keep us in perpetual disempowerment and financial struggle.

Choice + Action = Change

Choice is your first step. Making the decision to heal any outworn and undermining ideas you may be harboring about money is essential. But alone, it's just not enough. You also need to take action.

You see, there are many tentacles that may be holding you back. These tentacles are related to your mindset, your early influences, your community, your subconscious mind and your skill sets. So even if you mentally 'get it' that you need to make a change in how you value and charge for your services, until you get rid of the tentacles that hold you back, you may not make the kind of transformation you need.

Bankrupt Ideologies

Marie Antoinette and her gilded ilk throughout history didn't leverage wealth for the benefit of others. In fact, they didn't do anything but hoard it for their own best interests. This wasn't **because** of the money. Their gold didn't have some intrinsic power to mesmerize them into corruption and neurotic greed any ore than our modern dollars do.

It was their bankrupt ideologies that resulted in their incredible wealth (pun intended), at the expense of everyone else. And yes, it is still going on today. But not among Holistic Business Owners. Not among healers, visionaries and change agents who feel called to make a real difference with their skills and talents. Why should we stay in struggle when we know full-well the sorts of real problems money (in the hands of the good) can solve?

Over the last few millennia, our systems and our consciousness have been dominated by an ideology whose cornerstones have been hierarchy, oppression, dualism and scarcity. It has unfolded in our world in the form of vast material disparity between the proverbial 'Haves' and the 'Have Nots'. This ideology is now, blessedly, dying. And its death is being mid-wived by ... guess who?

Conscious Leaders with Money

In our world as it stands today, the power to create positive change is driven by the agreed currency of exchange: money. Yes, there are also barter systems and in-kind contribution schemes that can and do work. But for the most part, we are still living in a monetary economy.

This may well change at some point in the future. But for the moment, money is the system. We can rile against it. We can point out the false debt system and the lie of the Federal Reserve, but that doesn't change the fact that if you need food, clothing, a roof over your head, shoes for your kid or tires for your car, you will need *money*.

From early authors like Napoleon Hill to the likes of conscious leaders and influencers like Oprah Winfrey, Wayne Dyer, Louise Hay, Jack Canfield, Esther Hicks and Anthony Robbins, our new world is being led, facilitated, guided and mid-wived by those who have plenty of money. These are the business owners who leverage their personal and financial empowerment to help empower others, by spreading hope, inspiration and needed information. In other words, their empowerment is serving to transform our world.

All Hands (and Hearts) on Deck!

With all that name-dropping, you might be thinking, "Yikes! I don't want to be famous. I don't have the urge to make some huge impact, and I like my small business just the way it is."

Great! Glad to hear it, because we need all good hands and hearts on deck right now — in every nook and cranny of the globe, in every community and at every level of society. From Skipper to Deck Hand, no service should go under valued. And this means we need you to do more than struggle, more than just get by. We need you to thrive enough to serve to your fullest capacity.

We need *you* to know what it feels like to feel fully **fed** (in the energetic sense), fully **supported** (in the material sense) and fully **energized** (in the happy-wholeness sense) so that you don't burn-out, bail-out or waste your precious gifts. We need you to be free to stop giving away your energy, recovering from constant overwork, managing hand-to-mouth hassles, or running a life-sucking business that's little more than a low-paying job.

This is the time of the awakening and that means it's *your time*.

And no matter what our system of exchange may become in the future, right now we've got green stuff called money. To use it right, make it right and leverage it right, it's time to heal your mindset around it, do a data dump of ideological garbage, and move forward with a plan that will allow you to:

- ✓ Live your life's True Purpose
- ✓ Make a bigger difference (in your community and our world)
- ✓ Thrive!

A Workable Plan

A workable plan that can move you forward isn't some kind of business plan. It's not a document, nor a concept, a vision or Mission Statement. It's an internal shift. It's a Mindset.

In this time of great change and awakening, there are more and more people coming online. And I don't mean the world wide web. I mean folks who are tapping into a *source beyond the small-s-self*. It's the countless healers, energy workers, wellness practitioners, spiritual teachers, mentors and change agents. It's the Holistic Business Owners who are tapping into higher guidance, deeper wisdom and their own true purpose for being here.

This is a wonderful, exciting time to live if you are among those awakening to who you truly are! Wonderful, that is, until your vision, your sweet dream, your heartfelt intent comes slamming up against the physical world.

That's why it's essential to rid yourself of a toxic money blueprint. How? By developing an effective business mindset, reframing un-examined money mantras that keep you locked into a financial predicament, recognizing how Spiritual Bypass keeps you struggling, and learning how to market and sell so that you can begin to operate

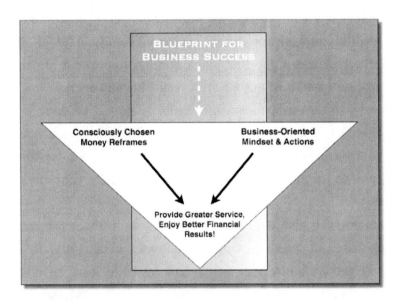

your business and your life from a place of financial as well as spiritual or personal empowerment.

A New Blueprint for Business Success
Get Your Business Groove On

Getting your business groove on means cultivating a *business-centric* mindset (as opposed to any of the four ineffective mindsets we looked at in Chapter 7) and reframing old money beliefs. When you do this, you'll be able to take different actions — which will lead to more fruitful results.

As these new mindsets, beliefs, and actions begin giving you better financial results, you will start to feel more at ease about your business and your life. You will find it easier to trust yourself as a business owner and enjoy your business, thanks to the proactive choices you are making.

This vision of what you want your business to be and do includes both the services you provide for others and, more importantly, the quality of life you want for yourself and your family. After all, didn't you go into business in the first place in order to create a life aligned with what you want to be and do with your time and energy?

It's easy to turn a business into a job. I know, I've done it three times. There's no joy at all when you have a fifty plus hour a week job that is your business, plus you have to run that business, pay for your own insurance (or go without), and of course, handle your marketing and sales.

When you get your *business* groove on, you'll find, as so many of us have, that your capacity to serve increases abundantly! In short, when you get your business groove on by cultivating an effective business mindset, reframing toxic money beliefs, and then taking different actions, you'll start to feel a whole lot better about every area of your life. As one of my mentors once said, "Money can't buy you happiness, but it can solve a *lot* of problems!"

Business Steps for Success

Before we dive into the Money Mindset reframes, I want to give you four Business Mindset antidotes to counter the four Ineffective Mindsets into which many Holistic Business Owners fall. These will serve as a reminder to keep you engaged in your work like a business owner committed to service and success!

1. **Treat your Business Like a Business.** This is your antidote for a Hobbyist approach to growing a business. When you treat your business like a business, you commit yourself to cultivating business skills, pricing your services based on value, and investing in the support you need for success.

2. **Claim Your Right to a Whole and Happy Life.** This is your antidote for the Holy Broke Helper. Remember that in order to live in this material world, you need to nurture spirit, mind, and body. And, love it or hate it, right now on planet Earth that means you need money. You have a right to thrive. More than that, you have an obligation, as a Holistic Business Owner, to make enough money so that you can step into leadership, wherever you may be called to do it. And that takes a level of material stability you cannot find by rejecting money on spiritual or moral principles.

3. **Take Consistent Action.** This is your antidote to "Attraction without Action" or Law of Attraction inspired passivity. In order to build a successful business, however you choose to define it, you want consistent momentum, particularly in the area of marketing and sales. Even if you are heading in the wrong direction, with momentum you can adjust your course.

4. **Leverage Debt for Growth.** This is your antidote for inappropriate, (vice-like) thrift. One of the biggest mistakes you can make as a business owner is to believe you can grow your business without investing in it. I don't just mean supplies or cheap-o advertising (read: flyers in the health food store). Investing in your business means developing yourself personally. It means investing in marketing. It means investing to get yourself ir

front of your ideal audience. And it means getting business mentorship. These things don't come free.

Ineffective Mindset	Says and Does	Stop and Change: Holistic Business Mindset
#1 Hobbyist "Our services are so precious that we are obligated to practically give them away!"	"I can't charge that much!" Attracts clients who can't afford services; operates on love offerings, very low pricing or sliding-scale, so never gets ahead.	"I charge for the value I offer." "I treat my business like a business. I price my services based on their value and I make money."
#2 Holy Broke Helper "It's easier for a camel to go through the eye of a needle than it is for a rich man to get into heaven."	"The greedy 1%!" "The love of money is the root of all evil." Lives in survival mode, barely scratching out a living, and wasting precious time on non-business activities.	"I claim my right to a whole and happy life. I need to thrive so I can help others." "An abundance of money is the vehicle by which I'm able to BE and DO more in the world."
#3 Attraction Without Action "If I build it, they will come because my *intention* will attract them."	"I'd rather have a root canal than *sell* my services!" "Selling is sleazy. People will think I'm pushy, tacky or rude!" Avoids the sales conversation and asking for the sale.	"I take consistent action toward building a business by developing sound sales and marketing skills." "I have a business, not a job. Good sales and marketing skills are essential *arts* that allow me to build a good business."
#4 Thrift is a Vice "I really need this for my business but I can't invest in it until I make the money *from* my business."	"I can't afford it right now." Chases freebies, sacrificing quality; wastes money on trial and error schemes rather than investing wisely. Gets exactly what was paid...nothing.	"I leverage debt for growth. I invest in myself and my business." "I invest wisely in my business so I can make money, and in turn, be able to reach and serve others."

RE: Visioning Your Inner Blueprint for Success

Cultivating your business mindset is a multi-pronged approach. You want to be sure you are learning the art and craft of running a business; you want to learn marketing principles; and you want to develop your sales skills. Like anything studied and practiced long enough, you *will* get proficient over time. But a business mindset alone will not get you very far if you are blocked by a toxic money blueprint. That's why Part III, Money, is the longest. It's this icky sticky money piece that holds back and drags down highly gifted, intelligent, and heartfelt business owners.

If you *really* want to make a difference — in the world, your community, your family or simply the quality of your own life — it's time to heal any "wounds" in your money mindset. This means deleting the old patterns, ideas and excuses, then replacing those undermining, inner conversations with a healthy blueprint for success.

When you do this, something miraculous happens. You begin to find, have, attract, and *take the right actions* to earn the money you need. And this of course, opens the door for you to effectively and abundantly do what you came here to do.

Today, we have many examples of people who started off dreadfully broke (including myself!). Some were even homeless, hungry ... but through healing our mindset around money, we managed to turn our lives around. Nothing made us more special or worthy than others in struggle. We simply told a new story, took different action and *found* (borrowed, earned, saved, re-prioritized) the money, in order to invest in ourselves and our vision.

Now, one thing I haven't included in my own story from struggle to success is the powerful role subconscious reprogramming played in my healing. In fact, without this, I'm certain I would not have had the courage or even the opportunity to invest in the mentorship, training, partnerships, and masterminds that propelled me to where I am today.

One of the most powerful of these was actually quite a simple process drawn from, of all places, an astrology book.[14] I took the concept from an exercise in the book, made some changes based on my own background as a martial arts instructor, business consultant and long-time meditator, and have since shared the process with clients and friends across the years.

Lives have changed :)

It's called "RE:*Vision*" because it's a way to RE*view* and RE*vise* your inner "vision" of who you are in the world.

The process itself involves some meditative or "stream of con-sciousness" journaling, some breath exercises, and an audio recording to ultimately RE:Vision yourself from the inside out!

As a way of saying "Thank You" for your good work in the world, I'd love for you to have access to this powerful, transformative tool too. It's the perfect accompaniment to this book, designed to help you shift subconscious habits of thought that do not serve you. To access and start the process right away, simply go to: http://spiritmindmoneybook.com/re-vision/. You can have it in a matter of minutes.

This process alone can help you set up a new operating system around abundance if you are really in struggle. When you pair it with the reframes below, you've got a powerful combination for transform-ing your relationship to Money, Service, and Success!

---

[14] *Measuring the Night: Evolutionary Astrology and the Keys to the Soul, Volume One.* Steven Forrest, Jeffrey Wolf Green, Jodie Forrest. Seven Paws Press, 2000.

Money Mindset Reframes

In Chapter 8 we looked at unexamined mantras that many of us default to saying when it comes to money. As I've argued, these are often the result of staying in struggle too long. Unexamined mantras *perpetuate* the problem because they allow us to avoid thinking through and addressing the real issues, such as investing in business growth, charging what your services or products (and your time!) worth, and dealing with false notions about what money is — and isn't.

Reframing these unexamined money mantras is a great way to get your conscious mind aligned with success, so that you can get on with your good work in the world.

So here are the reframes for these unexamined money mantras:

1. "I can't afford to invest any more money in my business." *Reframe*: "I value my business as a vehicle to help others and care for myself. Therefore I invest in the *business* of my business as well as my skill sets!"
2. "The love of money is the root of evil." *Reframe*: "Money expands who I already am."
3. "Money can't buy happiness." *Reframe*: "Money provides me with choices and greater freedom."
4. "I've got to keep my prices low or no one will buy from me." *Reframe*: "They don't yet see the value in what I am offering."
5. "I don't care about the money." *Reframe*: "When it comes to my business, it is equally about the money and the service I provide."
6. "It's so expensive." *Reframe*: "I don't want to make the effort to find money for that/this."
7. "I can't charge that much." *Reframe*: "I charge for the value my product/service provides."

Let's have a closer look at each of these reframes in turn.

1. Reframe for "I Can't Afford to Invest Money in my Business."

A business is not the same thing as a skill set. You can be the very best in the world at what you do, but if you want to turn that into a business which supports you, it will take more than modality certifications or educational achievement letters behind your name.

You'll need to value the importance of the business, put your money where your vision is, and invest cash in business growth. Whether that's learning business skills (like marketing and sales), investing in a website, an assistant, a coach or mentor (and likely, all of the above), without business skills and business support, you've got a service at best, and an expensive hobby at worst.

Your Prospects and Clients are a Reflection of ... YOU

Now we need to take this no-money mantra to a deeper level in order to see how you are showing up around money, when it comes to your business's needs. Are you making decisions about your business based on an "I don't have the money" set point? If you are, is it any wonder that the people showing up for you are singing that same song?

If the voice in your head is telling you that you can't afford to invest in the growth of your business, this is a *major* red flag. If you can't afford to invest in the growth of your business, you don't really have a business. I'm not saying that in order to run a successful business you have to spend wildly. Far from it. Investing in your business should be wise and strategic. But it *must* be done. Without investing in your business, you literally cannot grow.

Please also keep in mind that grabbing every freebie how-to you can get your hands on is *not* a business growth strategy. While there are plenty of valuable free tips and tools out there (too many), keep in mind that free incentive gifts are not *designed* to give you everything you need. If they were, the people giving them out would be put out of business darn quick!

Bargain Shoppers Get Crappy Deals

Another way of putting this is — Your Vibration Attracts your Results. What this means is that if you are showing up in your business looking to grow it on free tips or the cheapest investment possible, you'll reap exactly what you sow. The reason why bargain-shopping business owners don't stand much of a chance of real success is because if you are showing up in your life in a vibrational resonance of 'low budget,' then what's going to show up for you is C H E A P ... cheap crap, cheapie, penny-pinching clients, and crappy deals. A bargain shopper vibration will never lead you to abundance because bargain shopping isn't a business model; it's just an impoverished mindset trying to get ahead through squeaking by.

If you really want to grow your business, you'll have to invest. Strategically? Yes. One step at a time? Probably. But when it comes to anything related to business support or necessary equipment, be sure not to fall into the bargain basement mindset. Instead, reframe the conversation about your business investments like this:

"I value my business as a vehicle to help others and care for my-self. Therefore I invest in the business of my business!"

2. Reframe for "The Love of Money is the Root of Evil."

Money doesn't make one evil. Money expands who you are. If you value people over stuff, freedom over debt-slavery, personal wholeness over buying more flotsam, then you're not going to make decisions with your money that turn you into some kind of devil-worshipping greed weasel. In fact, if you are a person of integrity who values the betterment of all, then the more money you have, the more good you can do.

So let me ask you this. If you were to multiply your annual income by a factor of ten right now, what would you do with it?

- What percentage of that would you need to cover your basics?
- What percentage would you use to invest in building your business?
- What percentage do you need to pay off debt?
- What percentage would you want in order to bring more happiness into your own life (all organic food perhaps, or that family trip you've always dreamed of, a reliable vehicle, or yoga retreat). And finally ...
- What percent would you be able to use as a give-back?

What would you do with an extra $30,000, $50,000, $100,000 or more annually? How would that free you and your family to enjoy life more and be of greater service in the world?

So if you've been consciously or subconsciously buying into a belief that "the love of money is the root of all evil," I invite you to try this reframe:

"Money expands who I already AM."

3. Reframe for "Money Can't Buy Happiness."

Confusing money and happiness is indeed a big mistake. When people feel empty inside, a consumer-based society tells them at every turn that more "stuff" will fill the hole and do the trick. We all know this is a bunch of hooey.

However, the opposite side of the coin is equally as false. It is extremely difficult to live in the Western world when money is scarce. The increasing cost of living means that low-income reduces our quality of life, period. So while money, in and of itself, cannot "buy" happiness, it sure does solve a lot of problems. Your reframe therefore is ...

> ***"Money provides me with choices and greater freedom."***

4. Reframe for "I've Got to Keep my Prices Low."

When someone says to you, "I don't have that kind of money" in response to a product or service you are offering, but you *know* this is what they really need, what I'd like you to *hear* from now on is this. "I don't see enough value in the service/product you are offering to pay for it."

Let's be clear though, this doesn't mean your service or product isn't worthy. It only means that YOU have not brought across the benefits they will gain enough for them to *recognize* the value. In other words, you haven't developed your sales communication skills well enough just yet.

When you reframe such responses in this way, it puts you in charge of your conversations about money because you can evaluate and change your own message. You can look at what you are saying and not saying, how you are sharing the value of your offer, and how you can improve your sales skills.

If you find yourself attracting a lot of non-buyers who are saying "I don't have the money," instead of thinking you are charging too much or that your entire town is broke, I invite you to try this reframe.

"They don't yet see the value in what I am offering."

5. Reframe for "I Don't Care About the Money."

When you make your Soul Purpose Calling your actual work (read: business) in this world, it *has to be about the money* too. That's why it's very important to get clear about this — it *is* about the money. Without the money, there is no business. Without the business, you don't have bread on the table and the people you could have helped go without your gifts.

If you catch yourself thinking or talking about your business with an "it's not about the money" mantra, I invite you to reframe this with the following.

"When it comes to my business, it is equally about the money and the service I provide."

6. Reframe for "It's So Expensive."

This is where we really have to learn how to not take other people's opinions personally. It's a 100% losing proposition. So the next time you hear "that's too expensive!" from others (or yourself!) about a product or service, I invite you to hear the true statement, which has nothing to do with you.

Recognize that "expensive" is a perception, not an objective fact. Take the conversation out of the realm of expense and into the realm of value. When you hear, "it's too expensive" it's your job to clarify the value of what you are offering. Of course, this implies that you recognize the value of what you are offering, by reframing other people's judgement of your prices like this:

"They don't want to make the effort to find money for my offer."

7. Reframe for "I Can't Charge that Much."

As you disconnect your prices from a budget-oriented frame of reference and reconnect it to one focusing on the value of the transformation your product or services provide, pricing becomes a much less stressful issue. The next time you are pricing your products and services, I invite you to begin with the following premise:

"I base my prices on the transformative value it offers my clients."

Spirit, Mind and Money

Chapter Twelve
Your Most Important Investment

Putting Your Money Where Your Vision Is

In order for your business to grow beyond a mere sprout of an idea, you will have to invest in it. This is where courage may at times play a very big role. That's because some investments cost a lot. Whether it's a marketing opportunity to speak on someone else's stage because it will put you in front of your ideal audience, investing in a mentor, ad campaigns to get in front of the right people, or a website overhaul (among other things) ... if you want to make money, you're going to have to spend money. Anyone who tells you otherwise has never owned a successful business.

Investment Makes For Growth

Before you can attract clients who are willing to invest in your products, services, or programs, you have to be willing to invest in yourself and your business enough to be a vibrational match for the folks who would see the value — and have the money to invest — in hiring you. Why do I say this? Because I've seen it again and again in my own business and the lives and businesses of many others. People who radically improve their income quickly, do it by making a decision to change their Money Blueprint, then taking the immediate action of investing in business growth. (Remember my story from Chapter 7?)

True and lasting change began for me when I invested in it, by getting the support I needed. And it was BIG change. And it was FAST. I went from almost no income to a very healthy five-figures in (I'm not kidding) less than six weeks. And that was just the beginning! I took what was at the time a very scary risk. I put my money where my vision was and invested in high-level coaching, sponsorship opportunities, and a pricey website overhaul (complete with professional videos).

For you, that investment may look different, but I want to be clear here — when I say "investment" I don't mean acquiring another modality. I don't mean going back to school to garner another certification or diploma. For some people, that is indeed a part of the investment. But what I am referring to is investing in Business Skills, such as:

- Learning how to sell your services so you can have sales conversations and build your client base without feeling pushy or "salesy."
- Restructuring offers to add more value, so you can charge more per offer.
- Hiring a coach or mentor so that you take the right steps in the right order without reinventing the wheel of business.
- Hiring consultants, experts, and support professionals so that your marketing material, website, or programs are effective.
- Investing in exposure (through advertising, marketing, networking, sponsorships, and events) so that you can BE in front of your Ideal Clients and prospective customers.
- Learning how to position yourself as a professional or expert in your field so that you are the "go-to" in your industry or community.

"You have to spend money to make money." A Roman philosopher and poet names Titus Maccius Plautus said this back around 200 BCE. It's been used ever since to point out the fact that there are no get-rich-quick schemes. There are no short-cuts to building a thriving business. And there are certainly no free ways to create an income-generating business.

In this era of "think and grow rich" some of us get confused by belief versus action. We think if we just believe abundance is on its way, then be good and serve well, the money will come. But it won't. And here's why.

Unless you already have a Healthy Money Blueprint, you can't think your way into wealth. You have to change the default system. One of the best places to start with that change is by putting your literal money where your vision is — investing in the *business* of your business.

Money Management

Such a focus on money couldn't be complete without at least touching on the all-important subject of money management. Managing your money is key to keeping your business going. Just like driving a car blindfolded, you can't run a business and simultaneously avoid looking at your numbers.

Working with an accountant who understands your business goals and personal values is essential. These well-trained professionals are qualified to give you proper business advice. This being said, the below are some obvious recommendations for basic money management.

A Hot Date?

Have regular "dates" with your money. Carve some time out each week to look at what's come in and what's gone out. I have a date with my money at least once a week. I look at cash-flow, expenses paid, income for the week, and what remains of the month's projected expenses. I then compare that to what I allotted for each category for the month.

I also keep my business and personal expenses separate. This means I write myself a check once a week. It may sound silly to write a check from one account just to deposit it into another, but any accountant worth their salt would advise you the same. Don't mix personal and business.

Pay Yourself First

Before anything else gets paid, pay yourself first. If you don't, you'll find yourself in a never-ending "job."

Putting yourself first is part-n-parcel to success, literally and psychologically. After all, if you don't put yourself first, who will?

So when I say "pay yourself first," I don't mean to pay your personal bills first. I mean sock away a little money. Even if all you can do right now is save 10% of your monthly income ... do that. In time it will build, and in the mean time you will have the satisfaction of knowing you are, yep ... putting yourself first.

Welcome the Money

When money comes in, acknowledge it, celebrate it, welcome it. Money is a form of energy. If you want it flowing in your life, you need to make room for it and give it the energy of welcome. Your relationship to money does matter. The Law of Attraction *does* work. So be in appreciation of the money you have right now and then, each and every time new money comes in, give yourself a pause to say thanks. Better yet, do a happy dance!

Establish A Business Entity

When you have a business, the money you make and then reinvest in business growth is taxed differently than money you would make as an employee. But *only* when you set your business entities up correctly with the aid of an attorney.

One of my business mentors is Loral Langemeier. As a 5-time, New York Time Best-Selling author and internationally renowned wealth coach, Loral been helping people radically improve their financial lives for many years. To paraphrase one of her many salient points about money, she explains to her students that there are 2 ways people get taxed: When you are an employee, you pay taxes on your income, then use whatever is left to live on. But when you operate a business and put the right business entities in place (like C-Corporations, S-Corporations, LLCs, etc.), you use the money you make to grow and sustain your business first, and *then* pay taxes on what remains.

I am in no way qualified to advise you on how to do this. What I can say is that you would be well-served to consult an attorney and learn more about the importance of establishing the right corporate structure for your particular business.

The Bottom-Line Equation

The bottom line equation when it comes to making money is this — the more people you help get what *they* want ... the more you get what you want. If you are a Holistic Business Owner in service to your community or the world, then you, more than anyone, can recognize the profound truth of this statement. Place that statement in a money-based system of exchange and *voilá!* You allow financial abundance to flow into your life through your business.

Help more people get what they want = you get more of what you want.

Tying it All Together

Hi-Five! You've made it all the way to the end of what may have been an emotional challenging book. (Time for another organic cookie — yay!)

Now, before we finish, (and while you are nibbling that celebratory sweet), have a look at the table below. It presents you with two distinct choices for conducting your business and life moving forward.

From Toxic Money Blueprint	To Blueprint for Business Success
Outdated Money Beliefs	Holistic Business Owner with Money
Ineffective Business Mindsets	Mindset focused on Business Marketing & Sales for Success
Unexamined Money Mantras	RE:Visioning + Money Reframes = Positive Relationship with Money
Avoidance of Marketing & Sales	Investing in Strategic Marketing and Consistently Holding Sales Conversations
Frustration and Limited Results	Financial Rewards
Inaction and Fear as Debilitating	Action in the Face of Fear
Survival Mode: Scraping Out a Living	Business Success: Thriving and Helping Others

As we come to the end of the book, I'm hoping that much of what you've read resonates with you. I'd like to believe that I have brought home to you the importance of aligning yourself with the right side of the table (above). Those of us who have made the leap from left to right side can attest to the value of this move. Not only do we live better lives, we also have the financial capacity and energetic wherewithal to serve more people and engage our lives in a much greater capacity.

However, I'm acutely aware that making the leap from one side of this table to the other can feel huge. That's why I want to remind you once again how very important your work in the world truly is —

whatever it may be. To reiterate something I shared earlier in the book:

> *"If Spirit/God/Divine had the wherewithal to seed a vision and purpose within you, then the same force of All That Is absolutely has the wherewithal to provide a thriving living for you. But you will have to cooperate with that vision by developing the business skills you need and clearing up any contrary beliefs, habits and unexamined mantras that can block your success."*

This is really the crux of your way forward. We've come this far together. Let's keep going!

CONCLUSION
FEAR REVISITED

I began this book with a quote: "Where there's fear, there's power." When it comes to growing a sustainable business with authenticity and heart, expect to face fears from time to time. This could be fear around investing money for business growth or it could be fear around raising your prices, or learning to hold a sales conversation — and asking for the sale!

Fear sometimes accompanies overwhelm, when we are faced with a steep learning curve or many tasks to juggle. In our fast-paced world, fear can also arise when we need to make swift changes — in our business or in our lives. And of course, fear can arise like a demon when we know it's time to energetically "slay" our false, self-sabotaging beliefs about the intimate connection between *money, service,* and *success.*

The Intersection of Fear and Power

None of these fear triggers need be dangerous, nor debilitating. In fact, when you stay connected with the Spirit of your business — when you allow your vision and over-arching purpose to pull you forward — fear can be used like an internal power engine, driving you through, over or around the obstacles. That's what I mean by "where there's fear, there's POWER." Your power. Lying just beneath that thin veneer of fear.

It takes courage to run a business. Courage to face fear and recognize it for what it is ... a vibrational frequency based on thoughts, not reality. You can choose to feed fear by making decisions from a place of anxiety and scarcity. This enables fear to win — and eventually immobilize you. Or you can choose to let fear *feed* you, by using its energy to push you forward with courage and conviction.

With the strength of your **Spirit**, the skills of your **Mind**, and the alignment of a healthy **Money** mindset, it is indeed possible to face any fears you have and move through them. *For you, this book is not the end, it's the beginning of a new conversation about Service and Success as a Holistic Business Owner!*

About the Author

At 18 years old, Dawn found herself pregnant, single, and broke. Thanks to her family, she and her son didn't go hungry or homeless, but it was a long, slow climb out of low income and low expectations, despite her grit, determination, and education.

Today Dawn is the owner of Marketing with Heart, a business through which she provides content, copywriting, and mentoring services to Holistic Business Owners and leaders in the Personal Development arena. Dawn's consulting, training programs, and books are designed specifically for those who want to grow a thriving business with authenticity and heart.

Her services are responsible for equipping many heart-centered visionaries with practical business skills, and tens of thousands of dollars in increased revenue.

Dawn credits her success to healing her own "toxic" conversations about money, then investing in the mentorship and skill sets required to run a successful business.

She lives most of each year in Sedona, Arizona with her husband Doug. They spend their winters in Thailand and Southeast Asia.

For People Ready to Eliminate Financial Blocks to Business Success ...

RE:Visioning Your Inner Blueprint

A Special Gift from Dawn

RE:Visioning

"A Simple Way to RE*view* and RE*vise* your Inner "Vision" of Money, Service & Success, so you can Eliminate Financial Struggle, Make a Bigger Difference with your Gifts, and Grow a Business that Lets you *THRIVE!*"

RE:Visioning is a powerful method for eliminating harmful programming of any kind — at a subconscious level. The process is easy to do and ideal for the heart-centered visionary who longs to bring their gifts to the world in a bigger way, but struggles with financial limitation.

http://www.SpiritMindMoneyBook.com/re-vision

You can use the **RE:Visioning** process to ...

- ✓ Eliminate negative, subconscious programming about money .
- ✓ Effectively *do* what you came here to do, and thrive in the process.
- ✓ Swiftly transform your inner conversation around money so that it serves the highest GOOD of all.
- ✓ Set up a new *operating system* around abundance.
- ✓ Take effective, integrated action to earn the money you need.
- ✓ Transform your relationship to Money, Service and Success!

Grab Your Own Inner Blueprint for Success with a Complimentary Copy of the **RE:Visioning** Process

Access your copy and start your RE:Visioning right away, simply go to:

http://www.SpiritMindMoneyBook.com/re-vision

CPSIA information can be obtained
at www.ICGtesting.com
Printed in the USA
FFOW02n2131301015
18221FF